AMAZING
Rivers

100+ Waterways That Will Boggle Your Mind

JULIE VOSBURGH AGNONE & **KERRY HYNDMAN**

What on Earth Books

CONTENTS

**Sac Actun River,
Mexico, *page 40***

AUTHOR'S NOTE

Selecting which rivers to include in this book was not a simple task. There are so many rivers on Earth—each one unique and remarkable in its own way—but not enough pages for all of them. It was not a random selection, as I aimed for variety in geography and topic. My guidelines were clear: I would have room for only about 100 rivers from around the world, and each one needed to exemplify something fascinating, surprising, or awesome. I hope you enjoy discovering these amazing rivers as much as I did!

J.V.A.

WHAT IS A RIVER?

A river is a large, naturally flowing body of mostly fresh—rather than salty—water. Streams, creeks, brooks, and rivulets are generally shorter, shallower, and narrower, and often flow into rivers. Thousands of waterways crisscross the Earth's surface, flowing through all kinds of terrain—steep mountains, flat plains, lush forests, parched deserts, swampy marshland, and icy tundra.

Fresh water supports life on every continent of our planet—animals, insects, plants, and microscopic organisms all need it to survive. And so do humans. Throughout history people have settled near rivers for ready access to water. Many cities, towns, and rural communities still sit along waterfronts, and it's likely that there's a river not too far from your home.

LONGEST? THE NILE
Africa

The Nile is probably the world's longest river, flowing more than 4,100 miles (6,600 km) through 11 African countries. One of the earliest and most powerful ancient civilizations developed in Egypt beside the Nile. The ancient Egyptians, like peoples all over the world, depended on their river for food, water and transportation. Every year, the river flooded and deposited rich, dark soil along the flat land on both sides. The fertile soil made excellent farmland and today most of Egypt's population still lives near the Nile.

Fertile Land
Around 5000 BC Ancient Egyptians started to settle in farming villages beside the Nile. They raised livestock and grew crops on the flat land, called a floodplain.

Plentiful Food
People have been hunting animals, gathering food and catching fish along the banks, or sides, of the Nile for more than 10,000 years.

Transportation

To this day, the Nile is an important transportation route. In ancient times, people could count on the current to carry them downriver toward the sea and the winds to carry them upriver toward what is now Sudan. The laborers building the pyramids even transported the many tons of stone blocks they needed on the river.

Raw Materials

By about 4000 BC, fishermen and traders were building small boats using a flowering plant called papyrus that still grows in marshy parts of the Nile. Papyrus stems are lightweight and float, so boat builders tied bundles of the long reeds together to make the first rafts and watercraft. The ancient Egyptians used papyrus for more than boats. They also used papyrus for baskets, mats, sandals, and even writing paper.

HOW EXACT ARE RIVER LENGTHS?

It's not easy to measure a constantly flowing, twisting, shifting river. Many factors—like the decisions on where to start and stop measuring, the season, and tide levels—affect a river's length. That's why some official lists differ. For example, the Nile and Amazon Rivers are rivals for the world's longest, although the Nile tends to appear at the top of most lists.

SHORTEST? ROE RIVER
United States of America

In 1987, *The Guinness Book of World Records* officially awarded the title of "world's shortest river" to the Roe in Great Falls, Montana. At 200 feet (61 m) long, it is approximately the length of 4 city buses end to end. However, Lincoln City, Oregon argues that its D River is shorter than the Roe by 81 feet (24 m)—at least at high tide. In fact, several other rivers in the world could probably challenge the record if they chose. That particular world record has since been discontinued, however, so the Roe still holds the title.

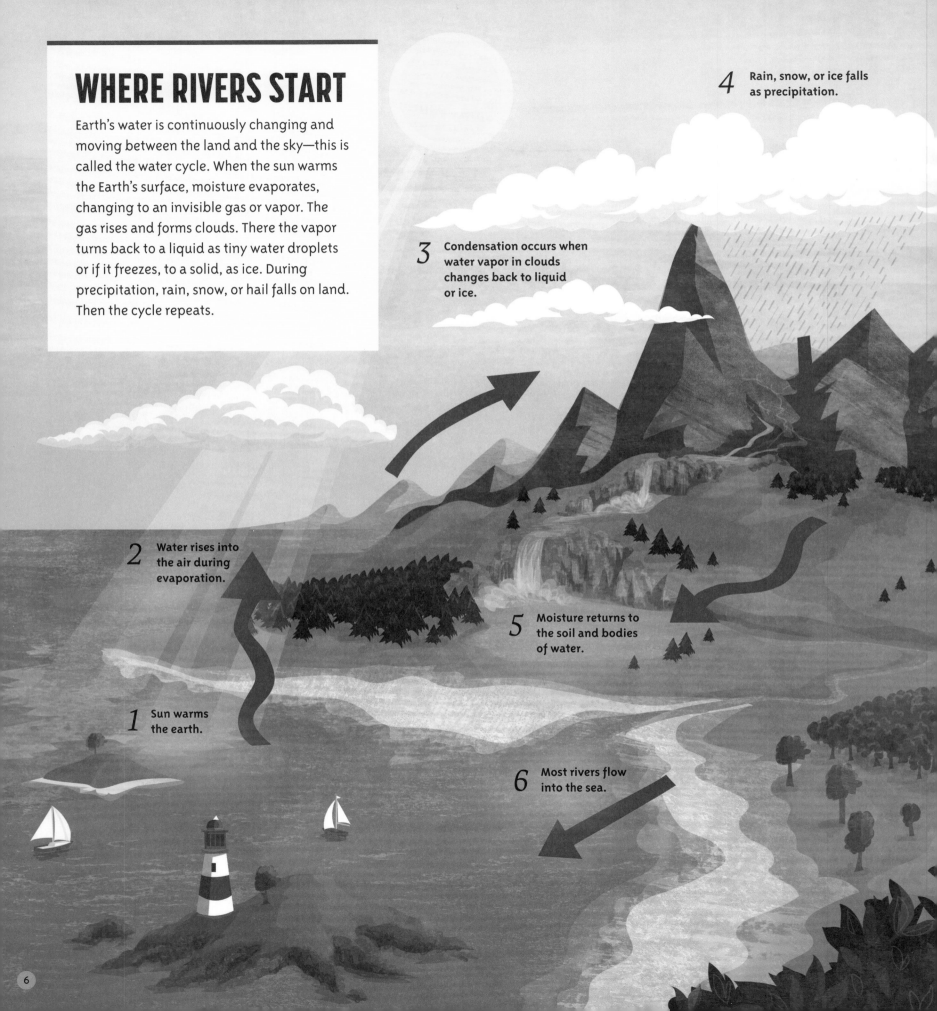

WHERE RIVERS START

Earth's water is continuously changing and moving between the land and the sky—this is called the water cycle. When the sun warms the Earth's surface, moisture evaporates, changing to an invisible gas or vapor. The gas rises and forms clouds. There the vapor turns back to a liquid as tiny water droplets or if it freezes, to a solid, as ice. During precipitation, rain, snow, or hail falls on land. Then the cycle repeats.

4 Rain, snow, or ice falls as precipitation.

3 Condensation occurs when water vapor in clouds changes back to liquid or ice.

2 Water rises into the air during evaporation.

5 Moisture returns to the soil and bodies of water.

1 Sun warms the earth.

6 Most rivers flow into the sea.

WHAT'S THE SOURCE?

Fresh water makes its way into rivers via different routes. The water may come from precipitation that has soaked into the soil, or from sources deep underground, or it can flow down mountainsides when rain falls or snow melts. A river always has a source, which is the place where it starts.

SNOW: SNOWY RIVER Australia

The Snowy River begins high on snow-covered Mount Kosciuszko, Australia's highest peak. When the snow melts in spring, the water naturally flows downhill, first as many small streams that then join bigger streams. These flow into the Snowy River as tributaries, feeding water into the river and causing it to grow as it continues its journey downhill.

GLACIER: RHÔNE RIVER
Switzerland and France

This river's source is the melting Rhône Glacier in the Swiss Alps from where it winds south through France to the Mediterranean Sea. (A glacier is a mass of ice that slowly moves down a mountainside or valley.) Visitors can actually walk inside the glacier through a cave carved right into the ice. The narrow tunnel glows brilliant blue as the light shines through the frozen walls.

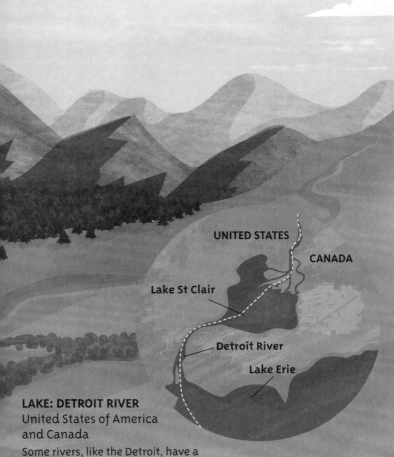

UNITED STATES

CANADA

Lake St Clair

Detroit River

Lake Erie

LAKE: DETROIT RIVER
United States of America
and Canada

Some rivers, like the Detroit, have a lake as their source. Lake St Clair feeds the river, which eventually flows into Lake Erie, one of North America's Great Lakes. The Detroit River has historically been an important route for shipping goods between Canada and the U.S. The city of Detroit sits alongside the river and is known for its automobile industry. In fact, a surprising number of cars—even a historic Ford Model T—have been dredged from the riverbed!

SPRING: AVON RIVER New Zealand

The Avon River starts as an underground spring that emerges in a suburban backyard and becomes a picturesque waterway as it courses through Christchurch, a major city on New Zealand's South Island. A popular activity on the river is punting in flat-bottomed boats. Instead of oars, punters move the boat using a long stick to push against the river bottom. Perhaps even more fun is hand-feeding friendly, 3-foot (1-m) long eels at the water's edge.

GOING WITH THE FLOW

The path that a river follows, called its course, often twists and turns around obstacles, rushes over steep sections such as rapids and waterfalls, and slows down in flat areas. The water flows along the river's course picking up more water from its tributaries and becoming wider and deeper. Most of that water eventually ends up in the ocean at the river's mouth.

WHAT IS AN OXBOW LAKE?

Sometimes the curve becomes very wide like a horseshoe (1) and the neck of the bend can narrow if the river starts to shift its course (2). Eventually the river may even take a shortcut, cutting off the loop and leaving behind a crescent-shaped body of water called an oxbow lake (3). The name comes from the U-shaped yoke used to harness oxen to a plow.

① ② ③

LIMPOPO RIVER
South Africa, Botswana, Zimbabwe, Mozambique

Some rivers curve back and forth across flatter terrain in loops called meanders. The Limpopo in southern Africa is an example of a meandering river—as it flows, the river erodes the outer banks and deposits soil and other material, called sediment, at the inner curves.

MARY RIVER
Australia

Australians call an oxbow lake a billabong. Several billabongs along the Mary River in Northern Australia are habitats for a vast number of rare birds, plants, and animals. The "green-haired turtle" is an endangered species found only in the Mary River. It got its name from the funny wig of green algae that grows on many specimens. With the ability to breathe through its rear end, it can survive up to three days underwater without surfacing.

RHINE
Switzerland, Liechtenstein, Austria, Germany, France, the Netherlands

The Rhine flows northwards from the Swiss Alps through five countries to the Netherlands, where it joins other rivers that empty into the North Sea. Some people assume rivers only flow from north to south, but they actually can travel in any direction, as long as it's downhill.

AMUR RIVER (HEILONG JIANG)
Russia, China, Mongolia

The Amur River forms a natural border between China and Russia. Many countries, states and provinces established boundaries around natural features like mountains, lakes, and rivers. That's one reason some borders on maps appear as wiggly lines. Countries that share a river may call it by different names. The Amur is also called Heilong Jiang in Chinese, meaning "black dragon river."

Brahmaputra

Ganges

BANGLADESH

INDIA

GANGES-BRAHMAPUTRA RIVER DELTA
India and Bangladesh

Most rivers eventually flow into the sea, sometimes spreading out in a wide triangular-shaped wetland area known as a delta. Here you can see where the Ganges and the Brahmaputra join to form the world's largest delta. This fertile region covers 41,000 square miles (105,000 sq km). Rivers in deltas become heavily braided, meaning the water divides into many channels that cross over and overlap like braided hair.

COLORADO RIVER
United States of America and Mexico

The constant flow of the Colorado River created the Grand Canyon, one of the world's natural wonders. The river cut through layer upon layer of rock over millions of years through a process called erosion. As it flowed, it picked up stones, pebbles, and soil, and this material scraped the banks and the river's bottom, or bed, slowly digging the over one-mile- (1.6-km-) deep canyon.

The Colorado River's erosion created this magnificent rock formation at Horseshoe Bend, so-called because the bend in the river is a tight, horseshoe-shaped meander. Like sculptors, rivers can carve amazing shapes from solid rock.

The Colorado River travels 1,450 miles (2,334 km) from the Rocky Mountains through several states in the U.S. and then into Mexico. The river's name is Spanish for "color red" as the water once appeared red because of the soil and rock it carried. Now only the upper part of the river runs red because dams downstream filter the water.

UNITED STATES

Colorado River

Lake Mead

Hoover Dam

Grand Canyon

Gulf of California

MEXICO

Bald eagle

In the 1930s, the Hoover Dam was built on the river between Arizona and Nevada. The 6.6-million-ton dam contains concrete, steel, pipes, valves, and other materials to harness the Colorado River. Some 21,000 workers labored under dangerous conditions over five years to complete the project.

Because 40 million people rely on the Colorado for its water and because there hasn't been sufficient snowfall to replenish water levels, demand is currently outstripping supply. The Colorado rarely reaches the delta where the river once regularly drained into the Gulf of California in Mexico. This has had devastating effects on crops and wildlife.

Havasu Falls spills into a clear blue pool on a tributary of the Colorado River in the Havasupai Indian Reservation in the Grand Canyon. The indigenous word *Havasupai* means "people of the blue-green waters."

A "bathtub ring" shows the previous water level.

Slowing the Colorado River's flow created Lake Mead, which serves as a reservoir to store fresh water. But the lake's water level has declined in recent years due to a combination of high demand, climate change, and drought. Vacationers often rent houseboats and explore rugged shoreline here.

PERILOUS OR PARCHED

When a river has too much or too little water, it can't drain efficiently. Floods occur when there is too much water and the river overflows its banks. A lack of water results in droughts and causes rivers to trickle or dry up. Both events can be dangerous to people and destructive to the environment.

LOA RIVER
Chile

The Atacama Desert in Chile is considered the driest place on Earth, yet suffered severe flooding in 2019 after a sudden rainstorm in the Andes Mountains. The parched soil around the Loa River simply could not absorb the heavy rain, and without warning, a flash flood swept through the region. Floodwater carried away everything in its path.

INDUS RIVER
Pakistan

During summer and early fall, heavy rains called monsoons are a regular part of life in many Asian countries. Monsoons bring much-needed rain, but can also cause catastrophic flooding. In 2010, the Indus River overflowed, killing an estimated 2,000 people and causing damage that affected more than 18 million others.

TIBER RIVER
Italy

Flooding around the Tiber River was common in ancient Rome and in response, master builders went on to develop one of the world's first drainage and sewer systems called the Cloaca Maxima, which translates as "greatest sewer." Historic signs around Rome still mark the high-water levels reached by the Tiber's floods over the past 700 years.

MURRAY-DARLING RIVER BASIN
Australia

Australia's longest river, the Murray, has recently suffered a serious drought, along with another major river, the Darling. These rivers form a large drainage area, or basin, that is critical to providing water for farms. Australia has historically had periods of natural drought, but scientists say climate change combined with overuse and poor water management have made the problem worse. In some places, the flow completely stops, causing water shortages and many thousands of fish to die.

SAND RIVER
South Africa

At Kruger National Park in South Africa, rivers can disappear during the dry season. Even so, elephants know that if they dig into the dry bed of the Sand River, they will find fresh water. An elephant can consume about 50 gallons (189 l) each day—equivalent to drinking a bathtub full of water!

MARIKINA RIVER
Philippines

Tropical storms called typhoons are another cause of flooding. Typhoon Ketsana (or "Ondoy" as it is known in the Philippines) brought high winds and torrential rain in September 2009. The Marikina River could not contain the flow, and a muddy torrent of water spilled into the streets of the capital city of Manila.

RIVERS OF MANY COLORS

The color of a river depends on a variety of factors, including the source of the water, the reflection of light from the sky, and any suspended material. Mud, sand, pollution, dead plant matter, or anything else in the water, such as minerals, could affect the color.

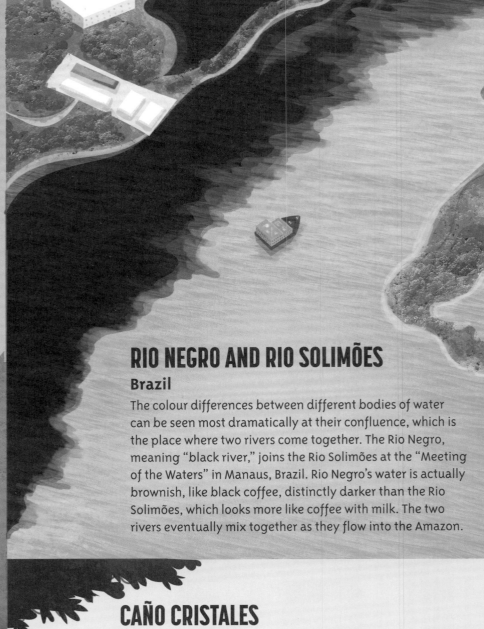

TARA RIVER
Montenegro and Bosnia and Herzegovina

The Tara is widely recognized as one of the cleanest rivers in the world and the crystal-clear blue-green water contains very little sediment. It's easy to see why people will drink right from the river. The area is a protected World Heritage Site.

RIO NEGRO AND RIO SOLIMÕES
Brazil

The colour differences between different bodies of water can be seen most dramatically at their confluence, which is the place where two rivers come together. The Rio Negro, meaning "black river," joins the Rio Solimões at the "Meeting of the Waters" in Manaus, Brazil. Rio Negro's water is actually brownish, like black coffee, distinctly darker than the Rio Solimões, which looks more like coffee with milk. The two rivers eventually mix together as they flow into the Amazon.

CAÑO CRISTALES
Colombia

The best time to see all the colors of the Caño Cristales at Serranía de la Macarena National Park in Colombia is during mid-summer and fall. That's when the bright-red riverweed is in full bloom. People call the multicolored river the "Liquid Rainbow." To protect this fragile environment, officials limit the number of visitors permitted to explore the site each day.

BLUE RIVER
Greenland

Kayakers seldom have the chance to paddle on the brilliant turquoise water of the Blue River because it's difficult to reach Greenland's remote Petermann Glacier. The Blue River is a rare supraglacial channel, meaning it sits on top of the glacier. Its pure water comes from melting glacial ice. Typically, melted ice creates lakes, which can refreeze, threatening to break up a glacier. But the Blue River helps drain lakes that form on the Petermann Glacier, transporting the water nearly 2 miles (3 km) to the sea.

YELLOW RIVER (HUANG HE)
China

The Yellow River, or Huang He, carries enormous amounts of sand-colored silt, or loose soil, downstream from the Huangtu Plateau region of northern China. *Huangtu* literally means "yellow earth." The light soil there erodes easily, and heavy rains wash the material into the water. The sediment can build up, which is why the river has a history of overflowing its banks. Considered the "mother river of China," the Huang He provides critical water resources to millions of people.

TIGRIS AND EUPHRATES RIVERS

Turkey, Syria, and Iraq

In ancient times, the Tigris and Euphrates Rivers supported Mesopotamia, a productive region that historians regard as the "cradle of civilization" because the world's earliest settlements and agricultural communities started to develop here more than 6,000 years ago. Towns and cities slowly grew and flourished because of these rivers.

4000 BC–today

Farmers tend palm trees that produce an abundance of sweet fruits called dates. Dates are an important crop in Iraq.

6000–4000 BC

Archaeologists have uncovered evidence that the practice of building ditches and canals for watering crops began in Sumer, in southern Mesopotamia. Sumerian farmers designed effective irrigation methods to divert river water to grow grains, fruits, and vegetables. The region's agricultural productivity had a major impact on the success of this developing civilization.

Black Sea

Caspian Sea

3200 BC
Sumerians recorded their history with a written language known as cuneiform. Instead of writing on papyrus like the ancient Egyptians did, they used a cut reed to press little triangle-shaped pictures into tablets made from the river's wet clay. Some tablets provide us with detailed records of daily life, like the numbers of the oxen and sheep that farmers traded.

Tigris River

Euphrates River

Baghdad

Mediterranean Sea

2100 BC
Each ancient city was centered around a temple called a ziggurat. The Ziggurat of Ur still stands in Iraq and has been partially reconstructed. Built with hundreds of thousands of sun-dried and baked bricks made with mud and water from the river, these multilevel structures are similar to Egyptian pyramids. Long stairways led to the top, where priests performed rituals close to their gods.

1300 BC
Sumerians invented the sailing boat and perfected it over time. Sails made of cloth allowed people to harness the wind to travel upstream. This changed the world because it allowed traders to more widely exchange goods and share knowledge in distant places. They traded grain, oil, textiles, jewelry, and pottery.

Sumer

Ur

Present Day
The modern city of Baghdad, Iraq sprawls along both sides of the Tigris. First settled as a tiny village more than 1,200 years ago, the metropolis has grown to a population of about 6 million. Iraq's 40 million people rely on the Tigris and Euphrates for 98 percent of their water. Yet blazing, dry summers and limited rainfall severely strain the river's water resources.

Persian Gulf

FAST FOOD

Rivers offer a generous bounty of food for humans as well as animals. Many rivers contain hundreds of different fish species, and tasty fish like river trout, walleye, bluegill, perch, and catfish are a primary food source. Some people assume that fish are the only edible food to come from rivers. But creative cooks know how to use local river resources to make tasty fare—from tiny grilled freshwater crabs in Thailand to Cajun-style alligator "bites" in the southern U.S.

BROOKS RIVER
United States of America

It's a brown bear buffet at Brooks River in Alaska, and fresh sockeye salmon is on the menu. Wild salmon spend most of their lives in the sea, but masses of them start to swim upstream in late June or July. Their purpose is to spawn, or deposit their eggs. The fish are determined, despite the 6-foot (2-m) high waterfall that slows them down en route. Somehow, hungry bears know that this is the best time and place to position themselves to grab a meal. This annual event attracts large crowds of spectators but bear lovers anywhere in the world can also follow the action via the live bear cam.

TONLÉ SAP RIVER
Cambodia

Cambodia's Tonlé Sap River is only 75 miles (121 km) long, but it's incredibly important because it fills a lake that millions of people in Southeast Asia depend on for food. During the rainy season, the river carries water from the massive Mekong River system to the lake—also called Tonlé Sap. In the dry season, the river reverses course and drains much of the lake back into the Mekong.

SHIMANTO RIVER
Japan

Fishermen net delicious freshwater shrimp in the Shimanto River. Restaurants serve the shrimp deep-fried and crispy. Cooked whole in its thin shell, these shrimps don't need to be peeled. Side salad with your meal? *Aonori*, an edible green seaweed, grows in slightly salty, or brackish, water near the Shimanto's mouth at the Pacific Ocean. *Aonori* is fried in batter, added to soups, or flaked and sprinkled like a spice.

VOLGA RIVER
Russia

When it comes to food, Russia is famous for producing caviar, or fish eggs. Caviar lovers will pay a high price and savor it as a delicacy. In a journey similar to Alaska's salmon, several species of sturgeon swim up Russia's Volga River— Europe's longest river—to spawn. Sadly, a dam now hinders them from reaching their spawning area, which has in turn seriously depleted the sturgeon population and Russia's caviar industry.

INDUSTRY...

In the late 1700s, factories sprang up along rivers—first across Europe and the U.S., then elsewhere in the world. Manufacturing processes depended on water to power equipment, cool machinery, and clean products. Plus, bringing in supplies and shipping out finished goods was more economical by boat.

HAIN RIVER
Belgium

Since ancient times, people have used the power of flowing water to run machines. This waterwheel in Braine-le-Château, Belgium harnessed energy from the Hain River as far back as the Middle Ages. Mills like this one ground wheat into the flour that villagers needed to make bread.

TURAG RIVER
Bangladesh

Workers at a textile mill in Bangladesh wash new denim in the Turag River, staining the water dark blue. One researcher estimates that it takes 2,000 gallons (7,600 l) of water to make a single pair of jeans. That's a lot of water to wash out the dyes and chemicals used in processing denim, and when the contaminated water goes directly into the river, it becomes toxic and the ecosystem suffers. Manufacturers and environmentalists are working to bring about the necessary changes to reduce the impact of the textile industry.

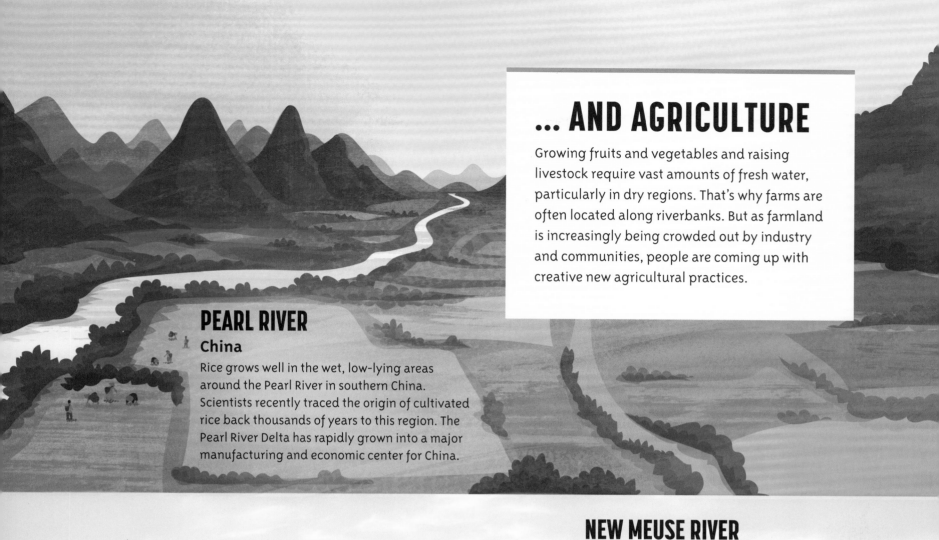

... AND AGRICULTURE

Growing fruits and vegetables and raising livestock require vast amounts of fresh water, particularly in dry regions. That's why farms are often located along riverbanks. But as farmland is increasingly being crowded out by industry and communities, people are coming up with creative new agricultural practices.

PEARL RIVER
China

Rice grows well in the wet, low-lying areas around the Pearl River in southern China. Scientists recently traced the origin of cultivated rice back thousands of years to this region. The Pearl River Delta has rapidly grown into a major manufacturing and economic center for China.

NEW MEUSE RIVER
Netherlands

The world's first floating dairy farm is operating on the New Meuse River in the Netherlands. Anchored to the riverbed, the three-story, mansion-sized farm can house 40 cows and produce 165 gallons (750 l) of milk and yogurt every day. This idea for "urban agriculture" comes from a trend to produce fresh food closer to cities in a more eco-friendly way. Robots are on clean-up duty and the manure waste is recycled as fertilizer.

The top floor has a greenhouse to grow grass, clover, and shade plants for the cows.

Milking stations and an area to prepare milk, yogurt, and cheese operate on the lower levels.

For a change of scenery, cows can wander over a ramp to a nearby field.

21

WATER HIGHWAYS

Long before people built roads, rivers were the primary transportation highways. Following waterways helped early explorers discover new trade routes. They found that the most efficient and cheapest way to transport passengers and heavy cargo was often by water. Even with modern rail, road, and air travel, people all over the world still rely on rivers as highways.

MISSOURI RIVER
United States of America

The Missouri is North America's longest waterway and holds great historical importance. In 1804–1805 explorers Lewis and Clark set out on the Missouri River at the request of U.S. President Thomas Jefferson. Their mission was to map a trade route and document the new U.S. Territory and native cultures. After reaching the Missouri's headwaters, they travelled on smaller waterways as far west as they could. Then they crossed the Continental Divide on foot and took canoes on the Columbia River all the way to the Pacific Ocean. During the difficult journey, they encountered grizzly bears and prairie dogs—creatures they'd never seen before.

Paddle Steamers

Steamboats known as paddle steamers started carrying passengers, goods and mail long distances on the Mississippi in the early 1800s. Steam-powered engines rotated paddle wheels, which churned the water to move the boats forward. Today historic paddle steamers carry crowds of sightseers.

Missouri River
Illinois River
Arkansas River
Ohio River
Tennessee River
Red River
Mississippi River

MISSISSIPPI RIVER SYSTEM
United States of America

The Missouri joins the "mighty" Mississippi River just north of St. Louis, Missouri. The name Mississippi comes from a native American language and means "great river," and it is well earned! The Mississippi is North America's second-longest river, flowing 2,348 miles (3,778 km) and stretching approximately 11 miles (18 km) across at its widest point. This river, together with the Missouri, Ohio, Arkansas, and other tributaries, forms the core of the Mississippi River System, which flows into the Gulf of Mexico. Most U.S. agricultural products travel along waterways in this river system.

MACKENZIE RIVER
Canada

Flowing north through Canada's Northwest Territories, the Mackenzie drains into the Arctic Ocean. The river is a vital transportation route, and not just for boats. Seaplanes carrying supplies to northern settlements often land on wide stretches of the river. During winter, the river and other bodies of water in the Mackenzie River Delta are covered with ice thick enough to support heavy lorries. Ice roads and ice bridges become a critical link to remote towns. Adventurous cyclists have even pedalled as far as 100 miles (160 km) on the frozen ice highway.

CHAO PHRAYA RIVER
Thailand

The Chao Phraya flows through Bangkok, Thailand's capital. Locals and tourists use the river to travel by ferry, water, taxi or river bus to work and major historic attractions. Floating vendors prepare and sell food from their boats.

ELBE RIVER
Germany

The massive *Hong Kong Express* container ship enters the Elbe River from the North Sea to dock at Hamburg, Germany. Fully loaded, the ship carries 13,000 truck-sized steel containers packed with cargo from Asian countries. The Elbe River is deep enough for the *Hong Kong Express*, but heavier vessels could get stuck. Shipping companies are trying to get permission to dredge, or dig up, the Elbe's riverbed to accommodate supersize ships.

RIVERSIDE LIFE

People all over the world appreciate and enjoy rivers in various ways because they offer recreational opportunities and places where families can relax and get close to nature. Festivals and major events frequently take place along rivers, often in honor of the river itself. Some rivers draw people for worship or to practice meditation.

GANGES India

During a massive spiritual festival called Kumbh Mela, Hindus bathe in India's Ganges and several other rivers. Named for the goddess Ganga, the "Mother Ganges" is held sacred by Hindus. Devotees consider the river's waters to be purifying and bathe in them as a cleansing ritual. Up to 120 million people can attend the weeks-long festival, which has been called "the world's largest gathering of humans."

SEINE RIVER France

Urban beaches are popping up along rivers in surprising places. These sunbathers in Paris are chilling at a sandy beach equipped with palm trees, umbrellas and deck chairs along the Seine River. There's no swimming in the river, but beachgoers can cool off in pools or enjoy ice cream from a vendor. The Paris tourism department wants to encourage people to stay in the city instead of escaping to the coast.

BRISBANE RIVER Australia

Barefoot waterskiing is a popular extreme sport on Australia's Brisbane River. Blisters aren't really a worry, but slicing through the water at 45 miles (70 km) per hour can be unpredictably dangerous. One skier nearly collided with a bull shark that leaped out of the river! Sharks are plentiful in the Brisbane River, so pay attention to those "No Swimming" signs.

NECKAR RIVER Germany

Spectators cheer as some 7,000 rubber ducks float downstream at the annual Tübingen Duck Race on the Neckar River in Germany. The first numbered yellow ducky to reach the finish line wins. That earns a gift certificate for the person with the matching number, and a big donation goes to a local charity.

YODO RIVER Japan

Every spring more than 400,000 people flock to Yodogawa Riverside Park in Kyoto, Japan to see the magnificent cherry blossoms. Visitors can walk through a magical pink tunnel formed by 250 flowering cherry trees. The park sits where three rivers join to form the Yodogawa—*gawa* is the word for river.

SPLASH ZONE!

Fast-flowing waters called rapids form when a river travels over uneven terrain or a series of rocky steps or dips. A waterfall forms when rushing water plunges over a steep drop-off or a cliff, and pours into a pool or river below.

A river's current is the movement, or flow, of water. The speed of a river's current varies depending on the terrain and the amount of water carried. Steeper inclines mean faster currents, so rivers generally run faster closer to their source and flatter terrain usually means a slower flow.

FUTALEUFÚ RIVER
Chile

The Fataleufú River in Chile has some of the most challenging rapids in the world. Whitewater enthusiasts love the excitement of rafting and kayaking the Fu's unpredictable currents. The water looks white because air bubbles in the fast-moving water are constantly being whipped up. Stretches of rapids on the river with nicknames like "Perfect Storm" and "Gates of Inferno" are especially exhilarating—and dangerous.

NIAGARA RIVER
United States of America and Canada

Tourists flock to the U.S.—Canada border to see spectacular waterfalls on both sides of the Niagara River. The river gains speed above Horseshoe Falls, on the Canadian side, travelling 25 miles (40 km) per hour before tumbling 188 feet (57 m) over the brink. The "Danger Zone" for treacherous rapids starts several miles upstream, but daredevils have risked their lives for the experience of going over the Falls. The first attempt inside a wooden barrel was in 1901 when a 63-year-old female schoolteacher survived the drop with just a few minor scrapes.

ZAMBEZI RIVER
Zambia and Zimbabwe

The Zambezi River drops into a spectacular waterfall credited as the world's largest curtain of falling water. The falls stretch more than a mile (1.6 km) between the African countries of Zambia and Zimbabwe. In 1855, explorer David Livingstone named it Victoria Falls after England's queen. But the locals had long been calling it *Mosi-oa-Tunya*, meaning "the smoke that thunders." Sunlight shining through the dense mist often creates rainbows over the falls. And on a clear night with a full moon, people can witness breathtaking "moonbows."

CONGO RIVER
Democratic Republic of the Congo and Republic of the Congo

The Congo is the world's deepest river and the second largest in discharge volume after the Amazon. It flows through western Africa into the Atlantic Ocean, draining an area that measures over 1.5 million square miles (4 million sq km.) Powerful rapids on the lower Congo look more like angry ocean waves than a river. Biologists have discovered that the fast, turbulent currents can create a barrier that forms separate habitats for underwater creatures on either side of the river. The Congo has hundreds of different types of fish and more unique species than almost any river in the world.

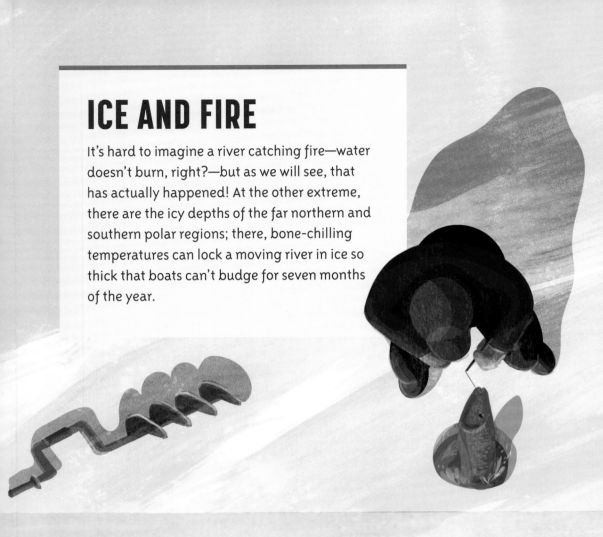

ICE AND FIRE

It's hard to imagine a river catching fire—water doesn't burn, right?—but as we will see, that has actually happened! At the other extreme, there are the icy depths of the far northern and southern polar regions; there, bone-chilling temperatures can lock a moving river in ice so thick that boats can't budge for seven months of the year.

LENA RIVER
Russia

Yakutsk, a city on Russia's Lena River in Siberia, has average winter low temperatures of minus 40 degrees Fahrenheit (-40°C). This is one of the coldest inhabited places on Earth and, during winter, the river is covered with ice over 6 feet (2 m) thick. But that doesn't stop fishermen. They drill a hole in the ice in the middle of the river, set up a little shelter to keep out the wind, and wait. With luck, they will catch dinner for a crowd: a Siberian giant taimen maybe, a type of salmon that weighs up to 66 pounds (30 kg).

DEE RIVER
United Kingdom

Imagine waking up and seeing lots of spinning ice pancakes floating on your local river. That's exactly what happened at the Dee River in Scotland. This bizarre occurrence is rare, and it requires just the right combination of temperatures and conditions. Pancakes form when slow, rotating currents, called eddies, form on the surface of the ocean or a river. Scientists think that the swirling motion rounds up ice or foam on the water's surface and colder temperatures freeze it into perfect pancake shapes.

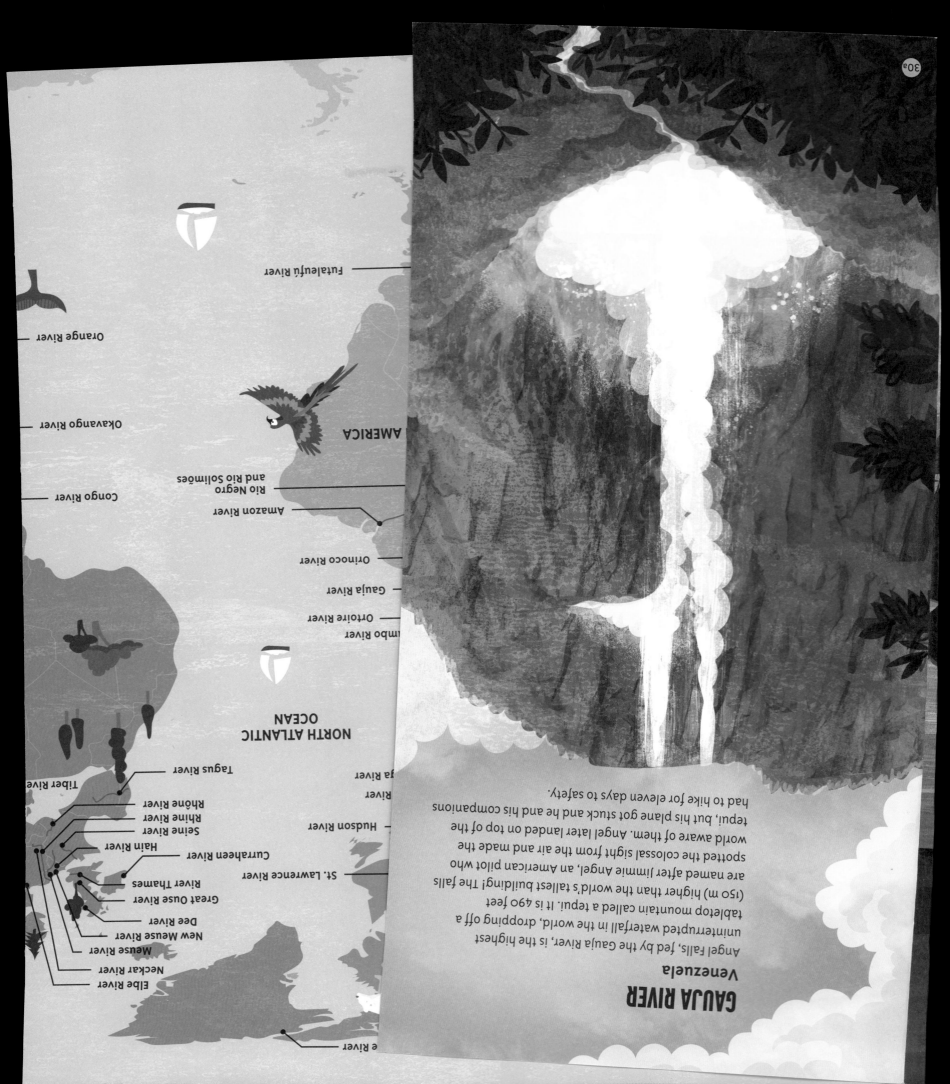

GAUJA RIVER
Venezuela

Angel Falls, fed by the Gauja River, is the highest uninterrupted waterfall in the world, dropping off a tabletop mountain called a tepui. It is 490 feet (150 m) higher than the world's tallest building! The falls are named after Jimmie Angel, an American pilot who spotted the colossal sight from the air and made the world aware of them. Angel later landed on top of the tepui, but his plane got stuck and he and his companions had to hike for eleven days to safety.

Futaleufú River

Orange River

Okavango River

Congo River

AMERICA

Rio Negro and Rio Solimões

Amazon River

Orinoco River

Gauja River

Ortoire River

...mbo River

NORTH ATLANTIC OCEAN

Tiber Rive...

Tagus River

Rhône River

Rhine River

Seine River

Hain River

Currabeen River

Great Ouse River

River Thames

Dee River

New Meuse River

Meuse River

Neckar River

Elbe River

Hudson River

St. Lawrence River

...ja River

...River

...e River

BOILING RIVER
Peru

This river's water is hot enough to cook an egg, although it's not quite boiling. At its hottest spot, the temperature is about 200 degrees Fahrenheit (93°C). The Boiling River flows deep in a remote jungle in Peru. It actually has hot and cold running water, starting out cold at its source and turning hot after thermal springs add scalding water. Apparently, small animals fall into the steamy river from time to time and die.

MEKONG RIVER
Thailand

Each year in late October, thousands of mysterious reddish fireballs float out of the Mekong River in Thailand and rise high into the air before disappearing. According to local folklore, these mysterious lights come from giant fire-breathing sea serpents called Phaya Naga. Scientists have posed theories suggesting flammable swamp gas is the real cause. Skeptics say the lights come from flares across the river. No one knows exactly, but it tends to occur during an annual festival, so many people come just to enjoy the spectacle.

CUYAHOGA RIVER
United States of America

The reason why a river might burst into flames is that there's flammable oil floating on top. It was chemical waste that led to a disastrous fire in 1952 on Ohio's Cuyahoga River that caused serious destruction in Cleveland. Even though fires were a regular occurrence on the Cuyahoga for decades, factories continued to dump toxic waste into the water because business was booming. When the thirteenth fire broke out in 1969, people finally took notice. That last straw ushered in big changes in U.S. environmental policies and industrial regulations.

Bald eagle

CAHABA RIVER
United States of America

The Cahaba River National Wildlife Refuge in Alabama protects animals and plants. It's an important habitat for many unusual species, 13 of which are found nowhere else in the world. The river has rare fish, snails, frogs, salamanders, and mussels that help feed bald eagles and many endangered bird species. The Cahaba lily, a type of spider lily, has delicate white flowers that open in the early evening and last only one day. Butterflies and fuzzy moths the size of hummingbirds help pollinate them.

Pipevine Swallowtail

Cahaba lily

Salamander

OKAVANGO RIVER
Namibia, Angola, Botswana

Unlike most rivers, the Okavango in southern Africa empties into a savannah, flooding part of the Kalahari Desert and creating a seasonal swamp. This flooded delta is a year-round home to lions and giraffes. From June to August, thousands of zebras, elephants, buffalo, and pink flamingos migrate from dry regions to the Okavango delta in search of water. It is a sanctuary for many threatened animals, including the black rhinoceros, a critically endangered species. There are only around 5,500 of these rhinos left in the world.

Black rhinos

AMAZON RIVER

Brazil, Peru, Bolivia, Colombia, Ecuador, Venezuela

At about 4,000 miles (6,400 km) long, the Amazon is considered the world's second-longest river—close enough to compete with the Nile for the title of longest. However, the Amazon is definitely the largest river when it comes to the sheer volume of fresh water it carries to the Atlantic Ocean. This measures a staggering 7 million square feet (200,000 m³) every second.

Scarlet macaw

Biodiversity Thrives

The Amazon River flows through the world's largest rain forest, which covers over 2 million square miles (5.5 million sq km). The rain forest has a warm, humid climate, with dense vegetation and an abundance of water. These create ideal conditions for wildlife to thrive. Millions of different species live here, making it one of the most biodiverse places on the planet.

Toucan

Blue morpho butterfly

Bird-eating spider

Fierce Predators

Giant river otters are some of the rarest animals in the Amazon Basin. They were once hunted for their sleek fur, and by 1971 only a dozen of them remained. Under protection, numbers have slowly increased to several thousand. With webbed feet and sharp teeth, these 66-pound (30-kg) mammals are fast swimmers and fierce fish-hunters. Their place as top predators in the Amazon River is challenged only by jaguars and enormous black caimans.

Some indigenous Amazonians live deep in the jungle far from civilization; a few have never had contact with the outside world.

Caiman

Giant river otters

Poison dart frog

Forest Fires

Farmers clear the rain forest to make space for crops and logging, even burning vast areas to the ground. Fires can get out of control, which kills many animals and plants and upsets the ecosystem.

Golden lion tamarin

Many animals, such as the brilliant golden lion tamarin and the scarlet macaw add flashes of color amid the thick green foliage.

Jaguar

Sloth

Creepy Critters

The Amazon region boasts its share of supersize animals that creep people out. It's legendary for 30-foot (9-m) green anacondas, 10-inch (25-cm) centipedes and 150-pound (68-kg) rodents called capybaras. Then there are the smaller but equally scary creatures like flesh-eating piranhas, bird-eating spiders, and poison dart frogs. However, every animal, no matter how threatening, has a unique place in this complex ecosystem.

Capybara

Catch the Wave

Expert surfers visit the Amazon for a rare chance to catch an "endless wave." A natural event called a tidal bore occurs only a couple times a year. High tides from the Atlantic Ocean create a powerful wave that rushes hundreds of miles upriver. Locals call it *pororoca*, which means "big roar," because you can hear it coming. Surfers love the experience, despite the risk of running into debris, poisonous snakes, and piranhas.

Green anaconda

Centipede

DANGER LURKS HERE

The Amazon isn't the only river that harbors dangerous animals. They're lurking everywhere—check these out—and be selective about where you swim! Remember, you're a guest in their habitat, so always be cautious and respectful of creatures that live in and around rivers.

GREAT OUSE RIVER
United Kingdom

Rivers like the Great Ouse in England are much cleaner now than in the past, so they're seeing a comeback of blood-sucking lampreys. These snake-like fish come equipped with round mouths full of tiny razor-sharp teeth. They feed on fish by latching on like a suction cup, piercing the skin, and sucking the victim's blood, which is why they're nicknamed "vampire fish." Lampreys will attach themselves to human swimmers too. Lamprey pie was once a favorite of British royals.

OMO RIVER
Ethiopia

And you thought the piranhas of the Amazon were terrifying! Another fish to avoid is the carnivorous goliath tigerfish, named for its dark stripes. This pointy-toothed 110-pound (50-kg) monster, found in parts of Africa, hunts in groups and occasionally attacks people, although humans are not their first choice of prey. If they're really hungry, they have been known to go after a crocodile.

DERWENT RIVER
Australia

A duck-billed platypus looks like a cross between a duck and a beaver. Smaller and skinnier than beavers, these furry critters use their webbed feet and flat tail to paddle around the Derwent in Tasmania and other fresh waterways in Australia. They're kind of adorable in a wacky way. But don't let the cuteness fool you. Sharp barbs on the males' back feet contain a potent venom and can inflict a nasty sting.

MARA RIVER
Kenya and Tanzania

Hippos have eyes set at the top of their heads so they can sink deep in the water while keeping a lookout. A hippopotamus may seem like a gentle giant because it spends most of its time lazing in rivers like the Mara in East Africa, but if you catch a glimpse of its sharp teeth, run! A wide "yawn" is a sign of aggression. These big fellas are surprisingly fast, and they've been known to break boats to pieces and even chase down lions and crocs. They kill about 500 people in Africa every year.

MAHAKAM RIVER
Indonesia

A giant freshwater stingray in Indonesia's Mahakam River looks more like an alien flying saucer than one of the world's largest fish. Rays reportedly weighing 800 pounds (363 kg) and estimated to be decades old feed on fish and other creatures from the river bottom. Their main defense is a poison-tipped whip-like tail that can penetrate bone. Fishermen rarely catch these stingrays because they bury themselves under heavy mud, creating a strong suction force. If hooked, they are strong enough to drag a boat or break fishing gear.

KATHERINE RIVER
Australia

It took Australian wildlife rangers ten years to finally capture a particular car-sized saltwater crocodile, or "saltie," in the Katherine River. There had been numerous sightings of the colossal croc over the years but it had evaded capture. It's common for these crocs to travel many miles up a freshwater river from the sea in search of food. It is unusual for one so large to hang around for so long. When these bad boys are near populated areas, they can pose a threat to public safety, so rangers relocate them elsewhere.

WEIRD RIVER RESIDENTS

Animals living in and around rivers have developed special abilities, habits, and features in order to thrive, some of which are pretty unusual. Known as adaptations, these characteristics help the animals survive the challenges of their environments.

YUKON RIVER
Canada and United States of America

The moose is the largest species in the deer family. But unlike most deer, moose stand 7 feet (2 m) tall at the shoulder. They have hefty bodies, distinctive faces, muscular shoulders, and broad antlers. Moose—with their thick fur—are well adapted to cold northern regions of the world, and the Yukon River area in Canada is home to a large population. Bears and wolves prey on moose, but they fend off attacks with their strong legs and large hooves or by swimming for miles across rivers.

DULCE RIVER
Guatemala

The Dulce River flows through a protected national park in Guatemala, so it's a great place to spot big, gentle manatees, also known as "sea cows". Primarily vegetarians, these marine mammals can grow to 1,210 pounds (550 kg). West Indian manatees live along coasts of eastern North and South America. Because they have no protective fat layer to keep them snug in winter, they seek out warm southern water in rivers and lagoons and sometimes near nuclear power stations. One of the biggest threats these creatures face is speedboats, which can injure or kill them in shallower areas.

KAMO RIVER
Japan

Japanese giant salamanders are active at night and almost never leave the water, which is why locals in Kyoto, Japan got the shock of their lives when a giant amphibian crawled out of the Kamo River in 2014. It's a harmless type of giant salamander that can grow to a length of over 5 feet (1.6 m) and gives off a spicy pepper smell when in danger. It has a wide mouth that stretches across the front of its head, but have no fear: it only eats insects, fish, and frogs and can survive weeks between meals.

DAINTREE RIVER
Australia

The southern cassowary is a long-legged blue-and-black flightless bird. A wild population lives near the Daintree River in the rain forest of northeastern Australia. Cassowaries have been known to attack dogs and even humans, and, if threatened, will fight fiercely with strong legs and razor-sharp toes. Should the cassowary need to escape, it can walk or swim across a deep river or even in the ocean. Fruit forms part of their diet, but they are unable to digest the seeds. Their droppings help plant more fruit trees!

Botos have very long, toothy beaks that they use to poke around for fish, turtles, crabs, and other river creatures.

ORINOCO RIVER
Venezuela and Colombia

The biggest and most unusual river dolphin species, the pink dolphin (also called the boto) lives in the Orinoco River and in waterways in the Amazon Basin and Bolivia. Scientists aren't sure exactly why it is pink, but its babies are born gray and adult males tend to be pinker than females. One theory is that the brighter color is due to scar tissue because the males fight a lot.

UNDERGROUND RIVERS

Some rivers are subterranean, meaning they flow underground for part or all of their length. In some urban areas, river systems have been intentionally covered up and built over. For example, although Londoners are generally unaware of the fact, more than twenty underground rivers flow beneath their city.

Subterranean rivers begin to form when rainwater seeps into the soil. Rain can be slightly acidic, so it slowly dissolves rock belowground. When it is soft rock like limestone, it wears away more quickly than other types. Eventually, the constant dripping and flowing water creates underground caves, winding passageways, and fantastic rock formations.

PUERTO PRINCESA RIVER
Philippines

The Puerto Princesa River is actually just above sea level but is considered an underground river because it flows beneath limestone rock. Tourists can take a 2.5-mile (4-km) boat ride into the cave through narrow passages and cathedral-like chambers. Guides with flashlights point out formations that resemble a horse, a mushroom, a jellyfish, and a naked lady. Fish and crabs swim in the river, but it's easier to spot the large bats flying overhead. Helmets keep visitors safe—from head bumps and bat droppings.

SAC ACTUN RIVER
Mexico

Sac Actun means "white cave," and visitors can see countless limestone caverns at this river in Mexico. The Sac Actun is part of a vast maze of underwater caves, which make up earth's longest underground river system, extending nearly 220 miles (354 km) to the Caribbean Sea. Snorkellers and divers find crystal-clear water here. Natural light often filters into the caves through numerous sinkholes, or *cenotes*, in the limestone roofs.

Archaeologists have found sacred objects, as well as animal and human bones, that ancient Mayans may have thrown in as sacrifices

THE (OTHER) NILE RIVER

New Zealand

There's another Nile River, and it's in New Zealand. This Nile flows inside a subterranean cave system, and black-water rafting is a fun way to explore fascinating rock formations inside. Unlike white water, this shallow river has slow-moving currents. At one point, you're lying on your back looking up at a dazzling display of glowworms lighting the cave ceiling like a starry sky!

YANGTZE RIVER (CHANG JIANG)

China

The Yangtze extends 3,915 miles (6,300 km), originating from glacier meltwater in China's Tanggula Mountains. It flows through spectacular scenery to the East China Sea in the Pacific Ocean.

The Yangtze is China's longest and most economically important river. It also ranks as the world's third-longest river. Its Chinese name, Chang Jiang, literally means "long river."

Three Gorges

A breathtaking scenic area known as the Three Gorges, is a natural and cultural destination named for the Qutang, Wu, and Xiling Gorges. Many tourists from all over the world visit this region to cruise, hike, explore caves, and take in the dramatic vistas from suspended walkways.

Wu Gorge

Qutang Gorge

Tiger Leaping Gorge

According to legend, a hunted tiger once escaped across a major tributary of the upper Yangtze by leaping onto a rock in the middle of the swirling rapids. The storied rock still stands at Tiger Leaping Gorge, one of the deepest canyons on Earth. Crashing water roars through the gorge, found near the Yangtze's source, so boats can't navigate this part of the waterway.

Tiger Leaping Gorge

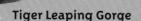

The Grand Canal

The Grand Canal connects the city of Hangzhou in the south and Beijing, China's capital, 1,100 miles (1,776 km) to the north. The Grand Canal also connects China's two most important rivers, the Yangtze and the Yellow River. This historic man-made waterway was built, starting in 468 BC, making it the world's oldest canal.

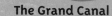

The Grand Canal

The Three Gorges Dam, the world's largest, was built at Xiling Gorge and stretches 1.5 miles (2.4 km) across the Yangtze River. At over 144 billion pounds (65 billion kg), it's the heaviest concrete structure ever built. It also has one of the most powerful hydroelectric stations on Earth.

Shanghai

Xiling Gorge

Three Gorges Dam

Shanghai

More than 26 million people live in the Shanghai urban area, making it the world's largest city. Dams and reservoirs upstream help control flooding and provide necessary fresh water for the region.

A massive ship lock at the Three Gorges Dam lifts ships up and down like an elevator lift between the river and the man-made lake above the dam. The Yangtze has a wide mouth so large ships can travel from here right to the sea.

Crayfish statue

Crayfish

A giant statue celebrates freshwater crayfish, which have become a booming business along the lower Yangtze River. People have developed a taste for these "little lobsters," which were once considered pests in China's rice fields. Now farmers cultivate the crustaceans in ponds and paddies, and China is the world's biggest crayfish exporter.

43

ENGINEERING FEATS

Rivers naturally tend to flow along a course of their own making. Throughout history, however, people have devised ways of controlling the course and even the direction of a river's flow, sometimes with remarkable success. Amazing technology and ingenuity have enabled engineers to build dams to create electricity, barriers to deter flooding, canals to divert water, and tunnels and bridges to get under and over rivers.

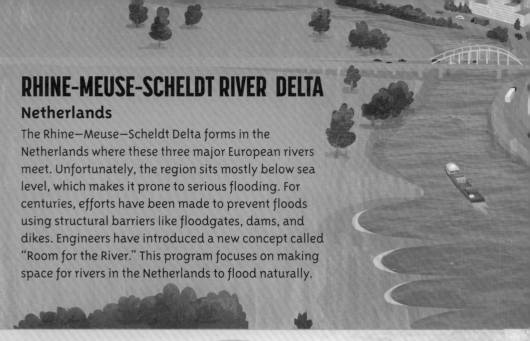

RHINE-MEUSE-SCHELDT RIVER DELTA
Netherlands

The Rhine–Meuse–Scheldt Delta forms in the Netherlands where these three major European rivers meet. Unfortunately, the region sits mostly below sea level, which makes it prone to serious flooding. For centuries, efforts have been made to prevent floods using structural barriers like floodgates, dams, and dikes. Engineers have introduced a new concept called "Room for the River." This program focuses on making space for rivers in the Netherlands to flood naturally.

TAGUS RIVER
Portugal

The Vasco da Gama Bridge in Lisbon, the capital of Portugal, is the longest in Europe at nearly 11 miles (17 km). Six lanes of traffic use it to cross the Tagus River at speeds that reach 75 miles (120 km) per hour. Dedicated to the Portuguese explorer of the same name, this sturdy bridge is built to last: architects designed it to withstand major earthquakes and hurricane-force winds.

KLANG AND KERAYONG RIVERS
Malaysia

The innovative SMART project, short for Stormwater Management and Road Tunnel, is designed for two purposes. Its main function is to divert floodwaters away from the city of Kuala Lumpur when the Klang and Kerayong Rivers overflow. The underground tunnel also provides a fast rush-hour route for thousands of cars every day. The tunnel has three levels: the top two sections carry traffic in opposite directions and water runs through the lower level during moderate flooding. But if there's heavy flooding, the tunnel is closed to traffic and the water flows through all three levels to a storage pond.

Traffic lanes

In major floods, traffic lanes are closed and all levels fill up.

Lowest level carries floodwater in moderate storms.

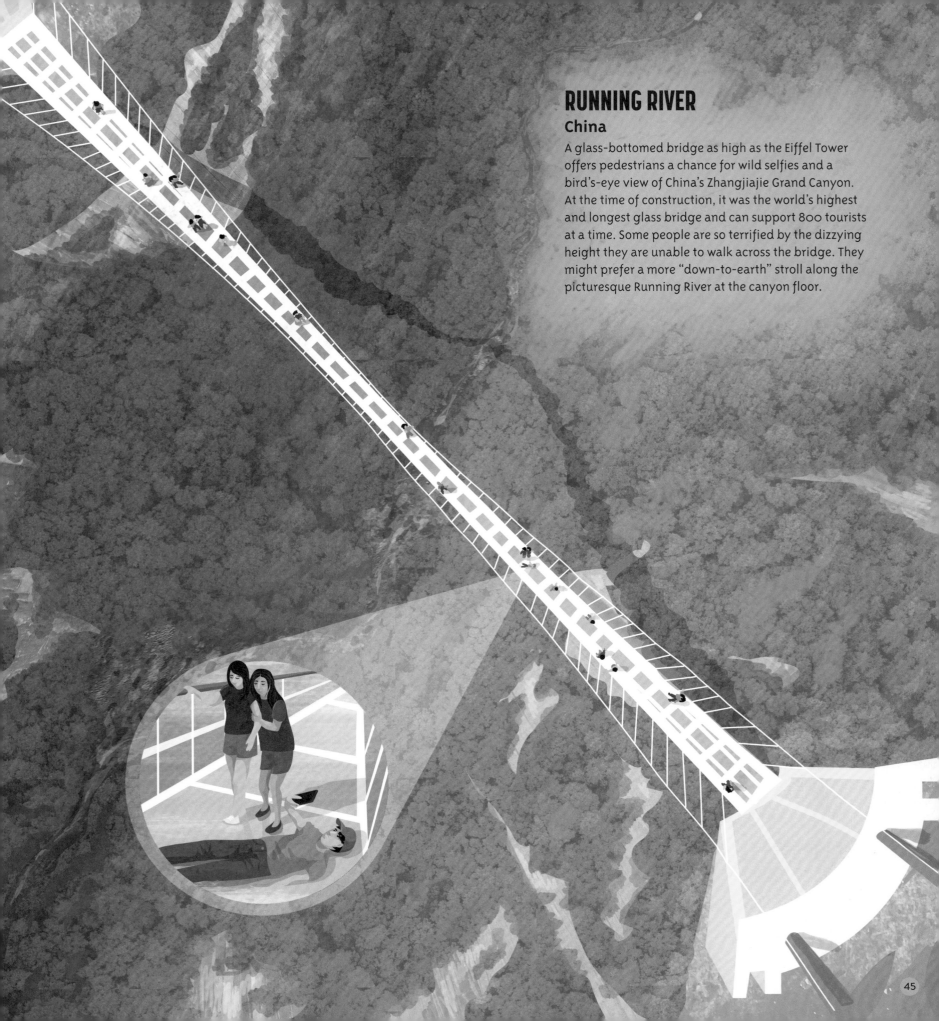

RUNNING RIVER
China

A glass-bottomed bridge as high as the Eiffel Tower offers pedestrians a chance for wild selfies and a bird's-eye view of China's Zhangjiajie Grand Canyon. At the time of construction, it was the world's highest and longest glass bridge and can support 800 tourists at a time. Some people are so terrified by the dizzying height they are unable to walk across the bridge. They might prefer a more "down-to-earth" stroll along the picturesque Running River at the canyon floor.

LI RIVER (LI JIANG)

The Li River, or Li Jiang, in China's Guangxi Zhuang region is a place of many natural wonders. There's no better way to tour the stunning scenery than from a boat cruising the 52-mile (84-km) stretch between the cities of Guilin and Yangshuo.

The unusual rounded hills surrounding the Li River are known as karst mountains. Over millions of years, water and weather erosion wore away the soft rock made of limestone and other minerals. It has carved underground tunnels and caves, and sculpted incredible rock formations. The Forest of Odd-Shaped Peaks is a favorite place to marvel at these fascinating works of nature.

A scene from the river is featured on the 20 Yuan banknote. A twist on the obligatory selfie is to get a photo of your hand holding the bill lined up in front of the same hills. First you have to find the right spot! Hint: It's at Yellow Cloth Shoal where there's a large yellowish stone that looks like cloth spread out at the water's edge.

Guides on modern tour boats filled with sightseers point out attractions along the river. For a quieter experience, visitors can also travel on traditional bamboo rafts.

Water buffalo come to the river to drink.

Reed Flute Cave is so named because thick reeds growing at the cave entrance were used to make flutes. Inside the colorfully lit cave are amazing geological formations. Pillar-like stalagmites jut upward from the cave floor, and stalactites hang from above like icicles. Every formation has a name, like Crystal Palace or Tower-Shaped Pine, and each has a fascinating legend behind it.

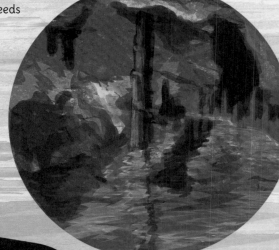

According to one legend, a beautiful group of seven green peaks overlooking the river are the Fairy Maidens Descending to the World. As the story goes, fairies from heaven visited the Li River at Yellow Cloth Shoal. The maidens enjoyed themselves so much they decided to stay forever.

FAMOUS LI RIVER HILLS

1. **Snail Hill** is hard to miss. With a long neck and green plants growing on its rounded "shell," the formation is easy to identify from any angle.

2. **Pagoda Hill** actually has a pagoda at the top! It was built as a place of worship during the Ming dynasty, between 1368 and 1644.

3. **Elephant Trunk Hill** looks like an elephant drinking from the river if you view it from the correct angle. Now see the reflection of the sun shining through the circle between the elephant's trunk and leg. It appears like a full moon is reflected in the water, which is why that circle is called Water Moon Cave.

4. **Fubo Hill** is named after a general from the first century AD and a temple was built here in his honor. It's also called Wave-Subduing Hill because it obstructs the flow of water.

Local fishermen work from small boats. Some use cormorants, large birds that can dive underwater, to help them catch fish.

Farmers along the Li River tend rice paddies.

THREATS TO RIVERS

Fresh water is a precious necessity that we sometimes take for granted. But we should be aware of the impact our actions can have. Increased demand from growing populations, climate change, industry, construction, and pollution all challenge the health of our planet's rivers. Poor water quality can seriously affect the well-being of humans and destroy the habitats of animals, fish, and plants in fragile river ecosystems.

Pollution enters rivers from a variety of sources and isn't always visible. The most obvious kind of pollution is litter, and people may not realize that the chewing-gum wrapper or drink can they discard by the side of a road will eventually make its way into a river. Sewage from human waste is another source of contamination, often carrying disease. Other threats come from agricultural runoff, industrial chemicals, and nuclear waste.

CITARUM RIVER
Indonesia

The Citarum River in West Java is one of the most polluted waterways on Earth. Floating debris, including tons of plastic waste, clogs the river. Many of the 2,000 factories located along the Citarum pump toxic chemicals into the water. People who rely on the river for drinking water are contracting illnesses. The military is helping clean up the river and enforce environmental regulations. Some people think the Citarum can't be rehabilitated. Others believe rivers have a natural ability to recover, but only if humans do their part.

JORDAN RIVER
Israel, Jordan, Lebanon, Palestinian West Bank, Syria

The Jordan River, mentioned numerous times in the Bible, has immense historical and spiritual significance. Everyone living in this dry area relies on it, but water rights have long been disputed in this politically volatile region. Neighbouring countries have dammed and diverted water from the river and its tributaries, causing the lower Jordan to trickle and damaging the ecosystem. There are positive signs that people are realizing that the only way to solve the crisis is to work together.

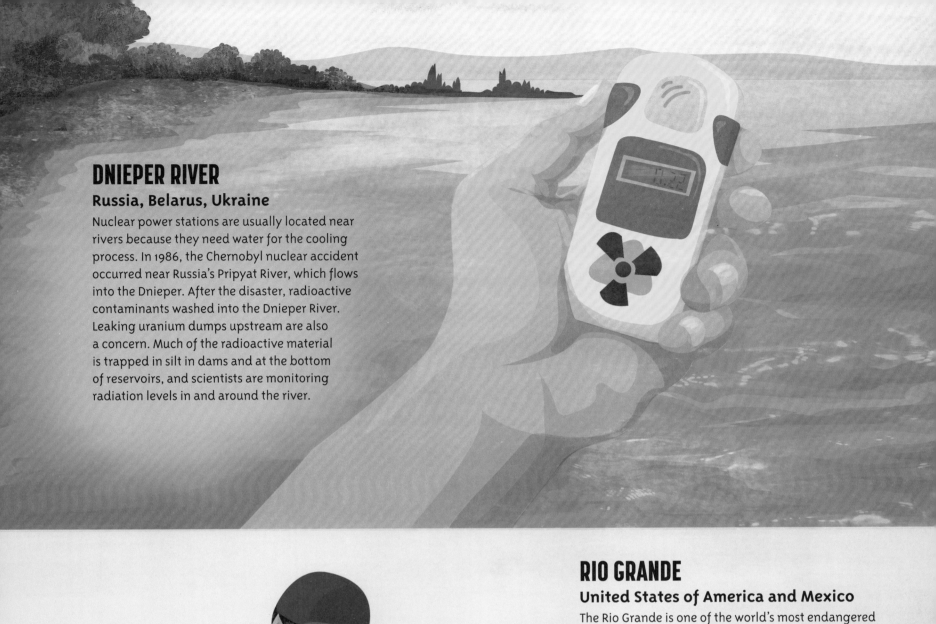

DNIEPER RIVER
Russia, Belarus, Ukraine

Nuclear power stations are usually located near rivers because they need water for the cooling process. In 1986, the Chernobyl nuclear accident occurred near Russia's Pripyat River, which flows into the Dnieper. After the disaster, radioactive contaminants washed into the Dnieper River. Leaking uranium dumps upstream are also a concern. Much of the radioactive material is trapped in silt in dams and at the bottom of reservoirs, and scientists are monitoring radiation levels in and around the river.

RIO GRANDE
United States of America and Mexico

The Rio Grande is one of the world's most endangered rivers. Overuse and poor water management are draining the river. On top of that, climate change is causing periods of drought, so some years the river never reaches its mouth at the Gulf of Mexico. Fish often lie dead in the dry, sandy riverbed. Environmentalists are working to relocate schools of endangered Rio Grande silvery minnows, a significant part of the food chain, before they become extinct.

RIVER INVADERS

Invasive species are organisms that can destroy an ecosystem. Such species are not native to a particular habitat and can cause harm because they compete with existing groups. Invasive species can include insects, snails, fish, snakes, frogs or larger animals like deer. They also include certain trees, shrubs, and other plants, and even fungi and disease-carrying bacteria.

River habitats are especially vulnerable to the bad effects of invaders because they are easily accessible and, once there, species can travel significant distances with the current. Sometimes invasive species hitchhike on boats or people release them into the water. If these invaders adapt well to their new environments and reproduce quickly, they crowd out the native animals or plants already established there—sometimes driving them to extinction.

CURRAHEEN RIVER
Ireland

The coypu, also called a nutria, looks like a giant rat with long bright-orange teeth. It can grow to 3 feet (1 m) long including its tail, and has webbed back feet for swimming. A few of these South American critters escaped from a pet farm in Ireland and started breeding in the nearby Curraheen River. People have since spotted coypu on other rivers. Coypu are considered invasive because they destroy riverbanks and crops and carry diseases. In countries where the coypu population is out of control, some people have suggested that the best solution is to eat them.

EDWARD RIVER
Australia

Several species of carp, which originally came from Europe and Asia, are taking over the Edward River and other rivers in Australia. Nicknamed "cockroaches of the waterways" by Australian fishermen, carp are becoming worldwide pests. They compete with native fish for food and ruin water quality. In many places carp grow fast and extremely large—up to 100 pounds (45 kg)! They are also jumpy. In some rivers hundreds of carp leap out of the water at once, accidentally clobbering boaters.

HUDSON RIVER
United States of America

You might think mussels are harmless. After all, people order them in expensive restaurants. Unfortunately, zebra mussels aren't tasty and have wreaked havoc in the Hudson River in New York and other waterways in the U.S. These mussels most likely traveled as hitchhikers on boats from eastern Europe. Having settled in riverbeds in massive colonies, they cause terrible damage because they attach to boats, pipes, docks, even rocks, and billions of them crowd out native species.

NAKDONG RIVER
South Korea

The Nakdong River is sometimes a lovely shade of green, but it isn't pretty. It's covered with algae, tiny organisms that multiply, or bloom. These algae blooms are actually a kind of bacteria, namely cyanobacteria. A combination of environmental conditions and stagnant water around dams encourages the growth of cyanobacteria and the result is a spongy green blanket that chokes the river of oxygen, kills fish, and contaminates drinking water.

AKAN RIVER
Japan

The northern snakehead, also called raigyo, is a long, skinny fish. It has a snake-like pattern on its sides and a mouthful of sharp teeth. After being introduced to rivers in Japan and elsewhere, they have been responsible for significant damage to the ecosystem. Snakeheads can survive out of water for several days and have the ability to wriggle over land to reach rivers, ponds, lakes, and drainage ditches.

RIVER TREASURES

People have long known that rivers hold all sorts of natural treasures like valuable metals, precious gemstones, beautiful rocks, and ancient fossils. Businesses and hobbyists mine rivers for such treasures worldwide. But before you consider filling your pockets while on vacation, find out about local laws that protect riverbeds and natural habitats. In 2019, a couple was thrown in jail for taking sand from a beach in Italy.

KLONDIKE RIVER
Canada

In 1896, miners found gold in a small creek flowing into the Klondike River in Canada's Yukon Territory. The discovery set off the Klondike Gold Rush, a mass migration of 100,000 hopeful miners wanting to stake their claim. Travel was rough and conditions harsh, and many never made it. For those who did, panning the river sand and surrounding area was hard work. The Gold Rush there was over by the end of the century when prospectors left for new goldfields. Tourists can still try panning for gold in the area, and some actually get lucky!

ORANGE RIVER
Lesotho, South Africa, Namibia

The Orange River runs 2,089 miles (3,363 km) from Lesotho through South Africa and then along the border with Namibia before emptying into the Atlantic Ocean. The history of South Africa's diamonds began in 1867 when a teenager found a rough 21-carat yellow diamond on the bank of the Orange River. The cut stone was named Eureka! Most mining operations moved away from the river, but today a few operate along the lower Orange River. Some even vacuum the seafloor at its mouth for precious stones.

PEACE RIVER
United States of America

Finding ancient fossils never grows old for expert geologists as well as amateurs. Florida's Peace River is a treasure trove of teeth, bones, and tusks. Millions of years ago, Florida was under the ocean. Layers of sediments buried creatures that had died, including megalodon sharks and now-extinct land animals like mammoths, giant sloths, and sabre-toothed cats. Erosion at the Peace River has stirred up some of these remains and fossil hunters sift the riverbed for keepers.

Megalodon's teeth were the size of a human hand.

KALU GANGA
Sri Lanka

The Kalu Ganga, or Black River, in Sri Lanka holds rubies, garnets, zircons, and sapphires in a rainbow of beautiful shades. Nearby Ratnapura is called the "City of Gems" because so many people here work in the gemstone industry. River mining along the Kalu Ganga is a simple and low-tech process, much as it has been for hundreds of years. Miners work at the river all day and carefully dredge up and sift through ancient gravel layers.

RANGITATA RIVER
New Zealand

Geologists love to hunt for agates and other minerals around rivers like the Rangitata in New Zealand. Agates look like boring bumpy rocks of various sizes, but when they're cut in half and polished, they're stunning works of art! Agates form in hollow pockets in a host rock, usually ancient volcanic lava. Every agate hides a surprise: a unique variety of colors, swirls, and patterns. Sometimes they even contain a cluster of glittering crystals.

SURPRISING FACTS!

Rivers are complex, fragile physical features that most of us seldom give much thought to, although some people are passionate about protecting them. In a few countries, rivers have even been recognized as "legal persons" with the same rights that humans have. It makes sense to think of rivers as nurturing, life-supporting beings because their health is critical to our own. Every waterway on Earth is unique and amazing in its own way.

YENISEY RIVER
Mongolia and Russia

Every June, villagers in Russia's far north celebrate the beginning of summer when a "tsunami"—or tidal wave—of ice from the Yenisey River begins to break up and piles form onshore. The Yenisey begins in Mongolia and flows through Russia into the Arctic Ocean. Huge chunks of thick ice in the river can create ice dams, blocking the water and causing floods. Explosives are regularly used to keep the river flowing. Boom!

WHANGANUI RIVER
New Zealand

When the Whanganui River was granted the legal rights of a person in 2017, some people thought it was a joke. The Maori, the indigenous people of New Zealand, were relieved, however, because their sacred river had been dammed, drained, polluted, and abused for many years. An old Maori saying is: "I am the river, and the river is me." They believe their ancestors live on in the natural world. Thinking about the river like a living being may make people think twice about disrespecting it.

ORTOIRE RIVER
Trinidad and Tobago

There's something in the water in the Ortoire River, and it glows. Swimming fish stir up a brighter glow. Somebody jumping in causes a splash that scatters like sparkly blue fireworks. This rare phenomenon occurs unpredictably at one spot along the Ortoire for only a few nights every ten or so years. The blue glow is believed to be caused by harmless tiny creatures called dinoflagellates. These remarkable organisms are bioluminescent, meaning they glow in the dark, but it takes billions of them to light up the river.

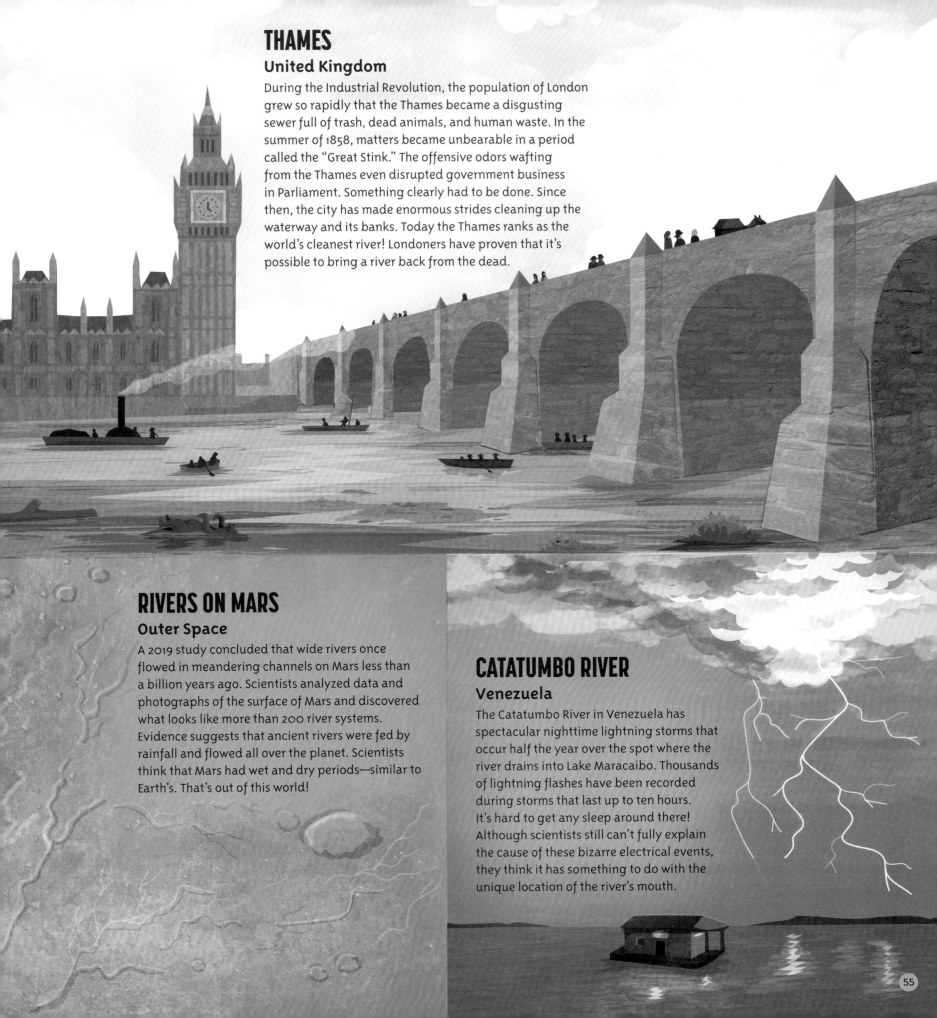

THAMES
United Kingdom

During the Industrial Revolution, the population of London grew so rapidly that the Thames became a disgusting sewer full of trash, dead animals, and human waste. In the summer of 1858, matters became unbearable in a period called the "Great Stink." The offensive odors wafting from the Thames even disrupted government business in Parliament. Something clearly had to be done. Since then, the city has made enormous strides cleaning up the waterway and its banks. Today the Thames ranks as the world's cleanest river! Londoners have proven that it's possible to bring a river back from the dead.

RIVERS ON MARS
Outer Space

A 2019 study concluded that wide rivers once flowed in meandering channels on Mars less than a billion years ago. Scientists analyzed data and photographs of the surface of Mars and discovered what looks like more than 200 river systems. Evidence suggests that ancient rivers were fed by rainfall and flowed all over the planet. Scientists think that Mars had wet and dry periods—similar to Earth's. That's out of this world!

CATATUMBO RIVER
Venezuela

The Catatumbo River in Venezuela has spectacular nighttime lightning storms that occur half the year over the spot where the river drains into Lake Maracaibo. Thousands of lightning flashes have been recorded during storms that last up to ten hours. It's hard to get any sleep around there! Although scientists still can't fully explain the cause of these bizarre electrical events, they think it has something to do with the unique location of the river's mouth.

GLOSSARY

BASIN
The area of land that is drained by a river system.

BILLABONG
An Australian name for an oxbow lake.

BIODIVERSE
Refers to a region that has a large number of different animal and plant species.

BRACKISH
Slightly salty water often found at the mouth of a river where fresh water mixes with seawater.

BRAIDED RIVER
Occurs when a river divides into multiple channels that cross over and overlap like braided hair.

CONFLUENCE
The place where rivers meet and flow together.

COURSE
The path that a river follows.

CURRENT
The movement, or flow, of water.

DAM
A barrier that blocks or reduces the flow of water.

DELTA
A broad triangle-shaped wetland where rivers spread out before they drain into the sea.

DIVERT
The practice of diverting, or changing, a river's course so some or all of the water follows a new path.

DROUGHT
A dry period with little rainfall that can cause rivers to be reduced to a trickle or dry up.

ECOSYSTEMS
Complex, intertwined communities of living things and their habitats.

ENDANGERED
Relates to species that are at risk of becoming extinct.

EROSION
A process caused by natural forces like water, wind, and glaciers that wears away, and reshapes the landscape over time.

ESTUARY
A wide area where a river meets the sea. The wide mouth of some rivers where fresh water meets and mixes with seawater.

FLOOD
The overflow of water from a river, lake, or ocean that covers land.

FLOODPLAIN
Flat land that is often flooded by a river.

FRESHWATER
Water that is not salty.

GLACIER
A mass of ice that slowly moves down a mountainside or a valley.

HABITAT
The place where an animal or plant normally lives.

HYDROELECTRIC
Refers to the production of electricity from fast-flowing falling water at the site of a dam.

INVASIVE SPECIES
Organisms not native to a particular habitat that compete with existing species and can harm an ecosystem.

IRRIGATION
Various methods of using water from a river to grow crops.

MEANDERS
The loops and curves that form when a river winds back and forth across flatter terrain.

MONSOON
Strong seasonal winds that bring heavy rain, which can cause devastating floods in parts of Asia.

MOUTH
The place where a river flows into the ocean.

OXBOW LAKE
A U-shaped lake that forms when a meandering river takes a detour and cuts off a bend in the river.

PRECIPITATION
Water that forms in clouds and falls to Earth as rain, snow, or ice.

RAPIDS
Fast-flowing waters that form when a river travels over steep, uneven land or a series of rocky steps or dips.

RESERVOIR
A storage place for fresh water, often a lake created by damming a river.

RIVER
A large, naturally flowing body of mostly fresh water.

RIVERBANKS
The land along the sides of a river.

RIVERBED
The channel through which a river flows; also refers to the bottom of a river.

SEDIMENT
Bits of sand and rock that are carried along by a river's current and settle on the river's bottom.

SOURCE
The place where a river starts. A source can be a lake, a spring, a melting glacier, or snowmelt from mountaintops.

SPRING
A stream of fresh water that emerges from underground.

TRIBUTARIES
Streams that feed into rivers or lakes.

WATER CYCLE
The process in which water is continuously changing and moving between the Earth and its atmosphere.

WATERFALL
Rushing water that plunges over a steep drop-off or a cliff and pours into a pool or river.

WHITEWATER
Describes a fast-moving current that looks white and frothy because air bubbles in the water are constantly being whipped up.

INDEX

SOURCES

WEB ARTICLES

Adhikari, Saugat. 'Top 11 inventions and discoveries of Mesopotamia'. Ancient History Lists. 20 November, 2019. ancienthistorylists.com/mesopotamia-history/top-11-inventions-and-discoveries-of-mesopotamia/.

Alberta Water Portal Society. 'How water is governed: What is Room for the River?'. albertawater.com/how-is-water-governed/what-is-room-for-the-river.

Apec Water. 'The Water Cycle: A Guide for Students'. freedrinkingwater.com/resource-water-cycle-student-guide.htm.

Backpacker South America. 'Caño Cristales, Colombia'. 10 January, 2019. southamericabackpacker.com/colombia/cano-cristales/.

Barnes, Angie. 'Rare Historical Artifacts are Everywhere at the Bottom of the Detroit River'. Boredom Therapy. boredomtherapy.com/detroit-river-treasures/.

BBC Wildlife Magazine. '7 fascinating facts about giant otters'. Discover Wildlife. discoverwildlife.com/animal-facts/mammals/facts-about-giant-otters/.

Better Meets Reality. 'Which Industries use the most Water'. 3 March, 2020. bettermeetsreality.com/which-industries-use-the-most-water/.

Biggs, Shannon. 'Rivers, Rights and Revolution: Learning from the Maori'. 13 February, 2017. Movement Rights. movementrights.org/rivers-rights-and-revolution-learning-from-the-maori/.

Bin Park, Soo. 'Algal blooms hit South Korean rivers'. 21 August, 2012. Nature International weekly journal of science. nature.com/news/algal-blooms-hit-south-korean-rivers-1.11221.

Blackwood, Gary L. 'Klondike Gold Rush'. August, 1997. HistoryNet. historynet.com/klondike-gold-rush.

Blankenbuehler, Paige. 'How best to share the disappearing Colorado River'. 20 December, 2018. High Country News. hcn.org/articles/water-how-best-to-share-the-drought-plagued-colorado-river.

Bradford, Alina. 'Moose: Facts About the Largest Deer'. 14 November, 2014. Live Science. livescience.com/27408-moose.html.

Bureau of Reclamation. 'Hoover Dam'. 12 March, 2015. usbr.gov/lc/hooverdam/faqs/damfaqs.html.

Bureau of Reclamation. 'Lewis and Clark: A Missouri River Adventure'. 1 July, 2015. usbr.gov/gp/lewisandclark/index.html.

Cahaba River National Wildlife Refuge. 'Wildlife and Habitat'. 2 May, 2018. U.S. Fish & Wildlife Service. fws.gov/refuge/Cahaba_River/wildlife_and_habitat/.

Cape Town Diamond Museum. 'The History of Diamond Mining and Diamonds in South Africa'. capetowndiamondmuseum.org/about-diamonds/south-african-diamond-history/.

Cassella, Carly. 'This Pink Turtle that Breathes Through its Butt is now Officially Endangered'. 12 April, 2018. Science alert. sciencealert.com/mary-river-turtle-green-hair-endangered-list.

China Highlights. 'The Three Gorges on the Yangtze River'. chinahighlights.com/yangtze-river/the-three-gorges.htm.

China Highlights. 'The Yellow River – 'Mother River of China'. chinahighlights.com/yellow-river/.

Cockburn, Patrick. 'Catastrophic drought threatens Iraq as major dams in surrounding countries cut off water to its great rivers'. 2 July, 2018. Independent. independent.co.uk/news/world/middle-east/iraq-water-rivers-shortage-drought-baghdad-war-isis-a8426766.html.

Craggs, Geoffery and Stubbs, Peter. 'The Ord River Irrigation Scheme – Charting a Course for Economic Success'. 19 October, 2017. FutureDirections international. futuredirections.org.au/publication/ord-river-irrigation-scheme-charting-course-economic-success/.

Curry, Andrew. 'The Box that Built the Modern World'. 25 July, 2013. Nautilus. nautil.us/issue/3/in-transit/the-box-that-built-the-modern-world.

Davies, Anne. '"The Darling will die": Scientists say mass fish kill due to over-extraction and drought'. 17 February, 2019. The Guardian. theguardian.com/australia-news/2019/feb/18/the-darling-will-die-scientists-say-mass-fish-kill-due-to-over-extraction-and-drought.

Davies, Guy and Joglekar, Rahul. 'Millions Congregate for Kumbh Mela festival in India, world's largest gathering'. 15 January, 2019. ABC News. abcnews.go.com/International/millions-congregate-worlds-largest-gathering-hindu-festival-india/story?id=60362673.

Dickinson, Hannah. 'How a Russian power plant almost wiped out the world's finest caviar fish'. 27 June, 2018. Independent. independent.co.uk/environment/russia-power-plant-extinct-caviar-pollution-overfishing-a8409526.html.

Dickman, Kyle. 'Evolution in the Deepest River in the World'. 3 November, 2009. Smithsonian Magazine. smithsonianmag.com/science-nature/evolution-in-the-deepest-river-in-the-world-147204782/.

EasyTourChina. easytourchina.com/photo-p10619-the-running-river-in-zhangjiajie-grand-canyon.

Engineering Rome. 'Water and the Development of Ancient Rome'. engineeringrome.

org/water-and-the-development-of-ancient-rome/.

Euronews. 'Radiation continues to "muddy the waters" in the Sea of Kyiv'. 22 April, 2016. euronews.com/2016/04/22/radiation-continues-to-muddy-the-waters-in-the-sea-of-kiev.

Fearnley, Kirstin. 'Weird & Wonderful Creatures: Amazon River Dolphins'. 6 September, 2016. American Association for the Advancement of Science. aaas.org/news/weird-wonderful-creatures-amazon-river-dolphins.

Fitzgerald, Roxanne. '"They're never this big": Rangers capture 600 kilogram crocodile after a decade-long hunt'. 9 July, 2018. The Sydney Morning Herald. smh.com.au/environment/sustainability/they-re-never-this-big-rangers-capture-600-kilogram-crocodile-after-a-decade-long-hunt-20180709-p4zqh7.html.

Fox, Esme. 'Puerto Princesa – a secret underground river in the Philippines'. 14 October, 2019. Rough Guides. roughguides.com/article/puerto-princesa-underground-river-palawan-philippines/.

German, Dr. Senta. 'Ziggurat of Ur'. Khan Academy. khanacademy.org/humanities/ancient-art-civilizations/ancient-near-east1/sumerian/a/ziggurat-of-ur.

Glanfield, Emma. 'Return of the vampire fish: Ancient Lampreys with nightmarish suckers filled with razor-sharp teeth make a comeback in British rivers and target swimmers'. 23 May, 2016. Daily Mail. dailymail.co.uk/news/article-3604264/Return-vampire-fish-Ancient-LAMPREYS-nightmarish-suckers-filled-razor-sharp-teeth-make-comeback-British-rivers-target-swimmers.html.

Grand Canyon National Park Trips. 'Havasu Falls and other Havasupai waterfalls near Grand Canyon National Park'. 9 April, 2019. mygrandcanyonpark.com/things-to-do/waterfalls-grand-canyon.

Hardach, Sophie. 'How the River Thames was brought back from the dead'. 12 November, 2015. BBC. bbc.com/earth/story/20151111-how-the-river-thames-was-brought-back-from-the-dead.

Hecht, Galen. 'Rio Grande is Dry, Despite Wettest Winter in a Decade'. 10 September, 2019. WildEarth Guardians. wildearthguardians.org/press-releases/rio-grande-is-dry-despite-wettest-winter-in-a-decade/.

Hinchliffe, Jessica. 'Bull Sharks are common in the Brisbane River so don't let your dogs go for a swim'. 23 January, 2019. ABC News. abc.net.au/news/2019-01-23/how-shark-infested-is-brisbane-river/10731866.

Holland, Eva. 'How to Build an Ice Road'. 14 June, 2017. Pacific Standard. psmag.com/environment/how-to-build-an-ice-road.

Ho Yen Yin, Sabrina. 'Supraglacial Lakes are not Destabilizing Greenland's Ice Sheets, Yet'. 23 May, 2018. GlacierHub.landsat.gsfc.nasa.gov/supraglacial-lakes-are-not-destabilizing-greenlands-ice-sheets-yet/.

iBan Plastic. '5 Cleanest Rivers in the World'. ibanplastic.com/5-cleanest-rivers-in-the-world/.

John, Finn J.D. 'Lincoln City's D River is part-time holder of a world record'. 14 June, 2010. Offbeat Oregon. offbeatoregon.com/H1006b_Driver.html.

Kessler, Rebecca. 'Musseled-Out Native Species Return to the Hudson'. 21 January, 2011. American Association For the Advancement of Science. sciencemag.org/news/2011/01/musseled-out-native-species-return-hudson.

Kiddle Encyclopedia. 'River Facts for Kids'. 11 March, 2020. Kiddle. kids.kiddle.co/River.

Kingtutshop. 'Ancient Egyptian Boats'. kingtutshop.com/freeinfo/egyptian-boats.htm.

Kornei, Katherine. 'Rare Glacial River Drains Potentially Harmful Lakes'. 14 June, 2018. Eos. eos.org/articles/rare-glacial-river-drains-potentially-harmful-lakes.

La Terra, Monique. 'Why You Should Visit Australia's Kosciuszko National Park'. 9 November, 2016. Culture Trip. theculturetrip.com/pacific/australia/articles/why-you-should-visit-australias-kosciuszko-national-park/.

Maher, Neil M. 'How Many Times Does a River Have to Burn Before it Matters?'. 22 June, 2019. The New York Times. nytimes.com/2019/06/22/climate/cleveland-fire-river-cuyahoga-1969.html?smid=nytcore-ios-share.

Mayo, Doug. 'Friday Feature: Floating Dairy in Rotterdam'. 3 June, 2019. UF: IFAS Extension University of Florida. nwdistrict.ifas.ufl.edu/phag/2019/06/03/friday-feature-floating-dairy-in-rotterdam/.

McCrone, John. 'Paradise for eels? Getting to know the secrets of NZ's new icon. 6 May, 2017. Stuff. stuff.co.nz/the-press/news/92191221/paradise-for-eels-getting-to-know-the-secrets-of-nzs-new-icon.

Metro Voice. 'Israel in environmental race to save the Jordan River and Dead Sea'. 3 January, 2019. metrovoicenews.com/israel-in-environmental-race-to-save-the-jordan-river-and-dead-sea/.

Morris, Ashira. '8 things you didn't know about manatees'. 26 November, 2014. PBS News Hour. pbs.org/newshour/science/8-things-didnt-know-manatees.

Mysterious Universe. 'Naga Fireballs: Swamp Gas or Divine Breath?'. 16 January, 2014. mysteriousuniverse.org/2014/01/naga-fireballs-swamp-gas-or-divine-breath/.

Nafisa Shahid, Sarah. 'Dark Flows the River Turag'. 8 June, 2018. *The Daily Star*. thedailystar.net/star-weekend/environment/dark-flows-the-river-turag-1587946.

National Geographic. nationalgeographic.org/education/.

National Geographic. 'Oxbow lake'. 10 June, 2011. nationalgeographic.org/encyclopedia/oxbow-lake/.

National Geographic. 'Waterfall'. 28 March, 2013. nationalgeographic.org/encyclopedia/waterfall/.

National Park Service. nps.gov/grca/index.htm.

National Park Service. 'People, Platforms, and Bears'. 21 July, 2015. nps.gov/katm/blogs/people-platforms-and-bears.htm.

National Park Service. 'Mississippi River Facts'. 24 November, 2018. nps.gov/miss/riverfacts.htm.

New Zealand Trails. 'Nile River Glow Worm Caves & Punakaiki'. newzealandtrails.com/news/nile-river-glowworm-caves-punakaiki/.

Nyffeler, M. and Pusey, B.J. 'New Zealand's fish-eating spider'. 18 June, 2014. Science Learning Hub. sciencelearn.org.nz/resources/673-new-zealand-s-fish-eating-spider.

Ogden, Lesley Evans. 'Why you should beware a laughing or yawning hippo'. 8 January, 2016. BBC. bbc.com/earth/story/20160108-why-you-should-beware-a-laughing-or-yawning-hippo.

Osaka Info: Osaka Convention & Tourism Bureau. 'Yodogawa Riverside Park'. osaka-info.jp/en/page/yodogawa-riverside-park.

Paleo Discoveries. 'Types of Fossils found in the Peace River area'. fossilhuntingtours.com/types-of-fossils-found-in-the-peace-river-area/.

Paris: Official website of the Convention and Visitors Bureau. 'Paris Plages'. en.parisinfo.com/discovering-paris/major-events/paris-plages.

Porto Montenegro. 'Tara river gorge – meet the turquoise treasure of Montenegro'. portomontenegro.com/blog/tara-river-gorge/.

Preceden. preceden.com/timelines/137589-nile-river-civilization.

Price, Larry C. and Debbie M. 'The Death of the Citarum River: Indonesia's Most Toxic Waterway'. 13 March, 2017. Pulitzer Center. pulitzercenter.org/reporting/death-citarum-river-indonesias-most-toxic-waterway.

Q-files. 'Ancient Egypt: Fishing and hunting on the Nile'. q-files.com/history/ancient-egypt/fishing-and-hunting-on-the-nile.

Ram Mohan, Kavya. 'Cloaca Maxima'. Atlas Obscura. atlasobscura.com/places/cloaca-maxima.

Roche, Barry. 'Concern over spread of rat-like coypu after Cork sightings'. 15 May, 2017. *The Irish Times*. irishtimes.com/news/offbeat/concern-over-spread-of-rat-like-coypu-after-cork-sightings-1.3083798?mode=amp.

Rosenberg, Matt. 'Major Rivers that Flow North'. 5 April, 2020. ThoughtCo. thoughtco.com/rivers-flowing-north-1435099.

Rosenberg, Matt. 'Oxbow Lakes'. 5 February, 2018. ThoughtCo. thoughtco.com/oxbow-lakes-overview-1435835.

Roth, Jeremy. 'Giant, spinning ice disc forms in Maine River'. 17 January, 2019. CNN Travel. cnn.com/travel/article/ice-disc-maine-presumpscot-river/index.html.

Row Adventures. 'Rafting the Futalefú River, Chile'. rowadventures.com/trips/futaleufu-river-rafting.

Sain Sr., Todd. 'Onyx River'. Our Breathing Planet. ourbreathingplanet.com/onyx-river/.

Schools Wikipedia Selection. 'List of rivers by length'. 2007. cs.mcgill.ca/~rwest/wikispeedia/wpcd/wp/l/List_of_rivers_by_length.htm.

Science alert staff. 'What Causes Brazil's "Meeting of the Waters"?'. 25 June, 2014. Science alert. sciencealert.com/what-causes-brazils-meeting-of-the-waters.

Scott, Michon. 'Heavy Rains and Dry Lands don't Mix: Reflections on the 2010 Pakistan Flood'. 6 April, 2011. Earth Observatory. earthobservatory.nasa.gov/features/PakistanFloods.

Seiff, Abby. 'When There are no more Fish'. 29 December, 2017. Eater. eater.com/2017/12/29/16823664/tonle-sap-drought-cambodia.

Shanghaiist. 'Hubei City puts itself on the map with 100-ton giant crayfish sculpture'. 5 May, 2018. shanghaiist.com/2015/06/17/giant_lobster/.

Smith, Paul. 'River Boats and Ferries in Bangkok'. Hotels.com. hotels.com/go/thailand/bangkok-river-boats-ferries.

Stiassny, Melanie. 'The Freaky Fishes of the Congo'. 20 May, 2008. National Science Foundation. nsf.gov/discoveries/disc_summ.jsp?cntn_id=111518&org=NSF.

Surbhi, S. 'Difference Between Estuary and Delta'. 31 October, 2017. Key Differences. keydifferences.com/difference-between-estuary-and-delta.html.

TCT Top China Travel. 'Cities and Provinces along the China Yangtze River'. topchinatravel.com/customer-center/cities-and-provinces-along-china-yangtze-river.htm.

TCT Top China Travel. 'The Longest Canal in China'. topchinatravel.com/china-guide/the-longest-cannal-in-china.htm.

The Associated Press. 'Water levels continue to drop at Lake Mead, Lake Powell'. 3 September, 2018. *The Denver Post*. denverpost.com/2018/09/03/lake-mead-lake-powell-drought-colorado-river/.

The Boiling River Project. boilingriver.org/.

The Nettlehorst School. 'Mesopotamian Achievements'. nettelhorst.org/ourpages/auto/2016/1/12/49314214/Achievements.pdf.

Thomlinson, Harvey. 'Go Down the Mighty Li River'. 2 July, 2017. *The Straits Times*. straitstimes.com/lifestyle/travel/go-down-the-mighty-li-river.

Thompson, Kelsey. 'Freshwater whipray'. Animal Diversity Web. animaldiversity.org/accounts/Himantura_chaophraya/.

Total Fisherman Guide Service. 'Tiger Fish'. totalfisherman.com/tiger_fish.html.

Travel China Guide. 'Li River'. 12 January, 2020. travelchinaguide.com/attraction/guangxi/guilin/li_river.htm.

Travel In Portugal. 'Vasco da Gama Bridge'. travel-in-portugal.com/attractions/vasco-da-gama-bridge.htm.

Travel Jael. 'The Complete Guide to Visiting Cenote Sac Actun'. 5 December, 2018. traveljael.com/the-complete-guide-to-visiting-cenote-sac-actun/.

Travel The Himalayas. 'The Tiger Leaping Rock'. 8 September, 2018. travelthehimalayas.com/kiki/2018/9/3/the-tiger-leaping-rock.

UNESCO. 'Okavango Delta'. whc.unesco.org/en/list/1432/.

United States Postal Service. 'Steamboats'. about.usps.com/who-we-are/postal-history/steamboats.pdf.

Unninayar, Cynthia. 'In search of sapphires: A behind-the-scenes look at gemstone mining in Sri Lanka'. 10 July, 2015. Jewellery Business. jewellerybusiness.com/news/in-search-of-sapphires-a-behind-the-scenes-look-at-gemstone-mining-in-sri-lanka/.

USGS science for a changing world. 'Rivers of the World: World's Longest Rivers'. usgs.gov/special-topic/water-science-school/science/where-earths-water?qt-science_center_objects=0#qt-science_center_objects.

USGS science for a changing world. 'Snowmelt Runoff and the Water Cycle'. usgs.gov/special-topic/water-science-school/science/snowmelt-runoff-and-water-cycle?qt-science_center_objects=0#qt-science_center_objects.

Victoria Falls Guide. 'Lunar Rainbow – Victoria Falls'. victoriafalls-guide.net/lunar-rainbow.html.

Wall, Mike. 'Mars had Big Rivers for Billions of Years'. 27 March, 2019. Space.com. space.com/mars-big-rivers-billions-years.html.

Waterman, Jonathan. 'The American Nile'. National Geographic. nationalgeographic.com/americannile/.

Whitley, David. 'Snakes, crocodiles and cassowaries: inside Australia's Daintree Rainforest.' 26 January, 2018. *EveningStandard*. standard.co.uk/lifestyle/travel/cape-tribulation-australia-what-to-do-what-to-see-a3750661.html.

Wikipedia. 'Ganges Delta'. en.wikipedia.org/wiki/Ganges_Delta#View.

Wong, Williams, Pittock, Collier and Schelle. 'World's top 10 rivers at risk'. WWF. March 2007. assets.panda.org/downloads/worldstop10riversatriskfinalmarch13_1.pdf.

Wow! Japan. 'How to Enjoy Shimanto River, the Last Clear Stream in Japan'. 8 October, 2017. wow-j.com/en/Allguides/shikoku/sightseeing/01383_en/.

WWF. worldwildlife.org.

WWF. 'The Amazon'. wwf.org.uk/where-we-work/amazon.

VIDEOS

Barefoot waterskiing, Brisbane River, Australia: youtube.com/watch?v=Jo1GQRndlF8 upi.com/Odd_News/2018/02/14/Water-skiers-close-call-with-flying-bull-shark-caught-on-camera/1571518635679/

Cataumbo River lightning, Venezuela: youtube.com/watch?v=7WfKgcnQFkI

Dolomedes fishing spider: youtube.com/watch?v=EbU6c-WJVI4

Duck-billed Platypus, Australia: youtube.com/watch?v=QNoQvJlmGdk

Eels, Avon River, New Zealand: www.facebook.com/chchdailyphoto/videos/eels-by-the-terraces-on-the-avon-river/10153667567702197/

Elephants digging for water in dry riverbed, South Africa: youtube.com/watch?v=jRYSaR_-Am8

Flooding in Atacama Desert, Chile: watchers.news/2019/02/08/massive-flooding-hits-atacama-desert-peru/

Giant river otters, Amazon River, South America: youtube.com/watch?v=uJWwaVim-Eo

Giant salamander, Kamo River, Japan: youtube.com/watch?v=KBh-EoiXjHU

Glowing Ortoire River, Trinidad and Tobago: youtube.com/watch?v=pO4-JA7Xhxo

Highlights from LiveCam, Brooks River, Alaska, US: explore.org/livecams/brown-bears/brown-bear-salmon-cam-brooks-falls

Invasive carp, Edward River, Australia: wsj.com/video/invasive-carp-plague-australia/0A65DD77-84BB-440F-A242-A90CC59C9EB2.html

Meltwater rivers, Greenland: youtube.com/watch?v=-EMCxE1v22I

Niagara Falls, United States and Canada: youtube.com/watch?v=ufZoZzDjjzE

Rhône Glacier, Switzerland: youtube.com/watch?v=2DWS5AVAvbY

Surfing pororoca, Amazon River, South America: youtube.com/watch?v=gMhNC2610Dg

The Stormwater Management and Road Tunnel (SMART Tunnel), Malaysia: youtube.com/watch?v=LU9aXDDGgbc

Yenisey River ice tsunami, Russia: https://www.dailymail.co.uk/news/article-7154639/Monstrous-ice-tsunami-powers-surface-Siberian-river.html

59

What on Earth Books is an imprint of What on Earth Publishing
Allington Castle, Maidstone, Kent ME16 0NB, United Kingdom
30 Ridge Road Unit B, Greenbelt, Maryland, 20770, United States

First published in 2021

Staff for this book: Sophie Yamamoto, Designer; Laura Marchant, Project Editor;
Andy Forshaw, Art Director

Library of Congress Cataloging-in-Publication Data available upon request

ISBN: 978-1-912920-26-6

Printed in China

10 9 8 7 6 5 4 3 2 1

whatonearthbooks.com